PRACTICAL SOCIAL WORK

Series Editor: Jo Campling

$$\boxed{\text{BASW}}$$

Editorial Advisory Board:
Robert Adams, Terry Bamford, Charles Barker,
Lena Dominelli, Malcolm Payne, Michael Preston-Shoot,
Daphne Statham and Jane Tunstill

Social work is at an important stage in its development. All professions must be responsive to changing social and economic conditions if they are to meet the needs of those they serve. This series focuses on sound practice and the specific contributions which social workers can make to the well-being of our society.

The British Association of Social Workers has always been conscious of its role in setting guidelines for practice and in seeking to raise professional standards. The concept of the Practical Social Work series arose from a survey of BASW members to discover where they, the practitioners in social work, felt there was the most need for new literature. The response was overwhelming and enthusiastic, and the result is a carefully planned, coherent series of books. The emphasis is firmly on practice set in a theoretical framework. The books will inform, stimulate and promote discussion, thus adding to the further development of skills and high professional standards. All the authors are practitioners and teachers of social work, representing a wide variety of experience.

JO CAMPLING

A list of published titles in this series follows overleaf

Practical Social Work
Series Standing Order ISBN 0–333–69347–7
(*outside North America only*)

You can receive future titles in this series as they are published by placing a standing order. Please contact your bookseller or, in the case of difficulty, write to us at the address below with your name and address, the title of the series and the ISBN quoted above.

Customer Services Department, Macmillan Distribution Ltd
Houndmills, Basingstoke, Hampshire RG21 6XS, England

D0609117

B32093

PRACTICAL SOCIAL WORK

Robert Adams *Social Work and Empowerment*

David Anderson *Social Work and Mental Handicap*

Sarah Banks *Ethics and Values in Social Work*

James G. Barber *Beyond Casework*

James G. Barber *Social Work with Addictions*

Peter Beresford and Suzy Croft *Citizen Involvement*

Suzy Braye and Michael Preston-Shoot *Practising Social Work Law (2nd edn)*

Robert Brown, Stanley Bute and Peter Ford *Social Workers at Risk*

Helen Cosis Brown *Social Work and Sexuality*

Alan Butler and Colin Pritchard *Social Work and Mental Illness*

Crescy Cannan, Lynne Berry and Karen Lyons *Social Work and Europe*

Roger Clough *Residential Work*

David M. Cooper and David Ball *Social Work and Child Abuse*

Veronica Coulshed *Management in Social Work*

Veronica Coulshed and Joan Orme *Social Work Practice (3rd edn)*

Paul Daniel and John Wheeler *Social Work and Local Politics*

Peter R. Day *Sociology in Social Work Practice*

Lena Dominelli *Anti-Racist Social Work (2nd edn)*

Celia Doyle *Working with Abused Children (2nd edn)*

Angela Everitt and Pauline Hardiker *Evaluating for Good Practice*

Angela Everitt, Pauline Hardiker, Jane Littlewood and Audrey Mullender *Applied Research for Better Practice*

Kathy Ford and Alan Jones *Student Supervision*

David Francis and Paul Henderson *Working with Rural Communities*

Michael D. A. Freeman *Children, their Families and the Law*

Alison Froggatt *Family Work with Elderly People*

Danya Glaser and Stephen Frosh *Child Sexual Abuse (2nd edn)*

Gill Gorell Barnes *Working with Families*

Cordelia Grimwood and Ruth Popplestone *Women, Management and Care*

Jalna Hanmer and Daphne Statham *Women and Social Work*

Tony Jeffs and Mark Smith (eds) *Youth Work*

Michael Kerfoot and Alan Butler *Problems of Childhood and Adolescence*

Joyce Lishman *Communication in Social Work*

Carol Lupton and Terry Gillespie (eds) *Working with Violence*

Mary Marshall and Mary Dixon *Social Work with Older People (3rd edn)*

Paula Nicolson and Rowan Bayne *Applied Psychology for Social Workers (2nd edn)*

Kieran O'Hagan *Crisis Intervention in Social Services*

Michael Oliver *Social Work with Disabled People*

Joan Orme and Bryan Glastonbury *Care Management*

Malcolm Payne *Working in Teams*

John Pitts *Working with Young Offenders*

Michael Preston-Shoot *Effective Groupwork*

Peter Raynor, David Smith and Maurice Vanstone *Effective Probation Practice*

Steven Shardlow and Mark Doel *Practice Learning and Teaching*

Carole R. Smith *Social Work with the Dying and Bereaved*

David Smith *Criminology for Social Work*

Gill Stewart and John Stewart *Social Work and Housing*

Christine Stones *Focus on Families*

Neil Thompson *Anti-Discriminatory Practice (2nd edn)*

Neil Thompson, Michael Murphy and Steve Stradling *Dealing with Stress*

Derek Tilbury *Working with Mental Illness*

Alan Twelvetrees *Community Work (2nd edn)*

Hilary Walker and Bill Beaumount (eds) *Working with Offenders*

Practice Learning and Teaching

Steven Shardlow
and
Mark Doel

MACMILLAN

First published 1996 by
MACMILLAN PRESS LTD
Houndmills, Basingstoke, Hampshire RG21 6XS
and London
Companies and representatives
throughout the world

ISBN 0–333–51634–6

A catalogue record for this book is available from the British Library.

10   9   8   7   6   5   4
05   04   03   02   01   00

Printed in Malaysia

To our parents

Contents

Preface

Social work education is changing very rapidly in the United Kingdom, in at least three important ways. First, there is increased emphasis upon learning about practice: the role of the practice teacher is ever more prominent and important – in our opinion, quite rightly so. Second, there is an increased emphasis upon the outcomes of learning, rather than the processes through which knowledge is acquired. Third, higher education is becoming accessible by a wider section of society – again, a trend that we welcome. However, available resources never seem to catch up with the breadth of these changes; there is always a shortfall. Practice teachers do not always get enough time or the equipment they need to provide good learning opportunities for students, nor do students, struggling to find good learning materials, always get the high quality of education that they deserve. No book on its own can correct such major difficulties. In this book we have tried to recognise the existence of these constraints upon both practice teachers and students.

Our intention in writing this book has been to provide a text that will be useful to both students and practice teachers. We hope for practice teachers, that the book contains some ideas about how to enhance skills in enabling students to learn about social work practice. The use of the word 'learning' is deliberate; our focus is on 'learning' not on 'teaching'. These two words, 'teaching' and 'learning' do not necessarily imply the same kind of activities. But we are anticipating the argument! We hope for students, that the book provides a guide about what to expect from a placement, so that students can negotiate, on a more equal footing, with practice teachers about how to maximise their learning. Students on social work

courses need to become, very quickly, sophisticated consumers of placements. We have seen too many students
who realise, only at the end of their final placement, what
the possibilities for learning really were. As the expan-
sion in higher education reduces the amount of contact
between students and tutors in class settings, the learning experience on placement becomes more unique. The
placement remains, for the moment, an opportunity for
individualised learning; with perhaps only one teacher to
each student. Students need to understand how to learn
about social work practice on placement and how to make
the most of the individualised learning opportunities they
are presented with – we hope this book will help.

In writing about and doing practice teaching, we have
both been forcibly struck by the similarities between class
based learning and learning about practice in social work
agencies. All too often, it seems as if these are regarded
as separate technologies of learning. There is a need for
an interchange – a dialogue between both contexts (class
and placement) for learning. In this book we seek to
promote that exchange by taking ideas that have traditionally been associated with one context of learning and
examining their applicability to the other context: the most
forceful example being idea of 'curriculum' – a complex
notion, fully described in Chapter 5. We have concen-
trated most upon the transfer from class to practice. In
developing these ideas our work experience has been very
influential. As, in the very recent past, we have both worked
in joint posts which have included, university teaching,
research, local authority social work practice and being a
practice teacher. Holding various roles simultaneously has
been a tremendous advantage in allowing us to see possible connections, similarities and differences between class
based and agency based opportunities and structures for
learning.

We recognise that some of the terms used in the book
will be unfamiliar. Also, that they carry very specific meanings in some contexts. Hence we have highlighted key
terms and when key ideas or concepts are first introduced,
we have provided a definition.

Using language that adequately reflects the degree of diversity in our society is problematic. We wholeheartedly affirm and recognise the multiplicity of experience in modern British society and wish to use language that is accessible and acceptable to all whatever their background. As far as possible we have not used the pronouns 'he' or 'she' generically: 'he' is unacceptable, it excludes women; using 'she' is unacceptable since it excludes men – its usage does not rectify a historical imbalance in terminology, but perpetuates a new exclusion. Therefore we have chosen to use the plural 'they' wherever possible. It may not always be strictly grammatically correct, but it is not gender specific.

Finally we have always believed that learning should be fun – if it is not there is something wrong.

STEVEN SHARDLOW
MARK DOEL

Acknowledgements

This book began life as a series of ideas that developed out of a small course on practice learning, held each spring in Sheffield for about six years. We owe a considerable debt to all who attended the course, from whom we learned much, in enjoyable debate, about how to achieve high quality practice learning. More recently, we have worked with a team of colleagues developing other courses in practice learning. We wish to thank them, Janet Atkinson, Yvonne Channer, David Henry, Philip Proctor, Catherine Sawdon, David Sawdon and Janet Williams, for their enthusiasm and inspiration. Many other people have influenced our thinking and we are grateful to them all. We also offer thanks to Jo Campling for her forbearance during the gestation of the book.

We wish to thank the editor of *Social Work Education* for allowing us to use material which was previously published in that journal. A revised version of part of our paper, 'Examination by Triangulation: A model for practice teaching', forms a section of Chapter 7. We also wish to thank Gower for allowing us to use an extract from *Social Work Practice* in Chapter 6.

STEVEN SHARDLOW
MARK DOEL

Part I

Contexts

... an exploration of the context underpinning practice learning

1

Beginnings . . .

'Where shall I begin, please your Majesty?' he asked.
'Begin at the beginning' the King said, gravely, 'and go
on till you come to the end: then stop.'
(Lewis Carroll, *Alice in Wonderland*, Chapter 12)

Summary

This chapter introduces some of the key ideas and assumptions contained in the book. There is also a summary of each chapter.

Introduction

Learning about how to *do* social work usually requires that students spend a period of time on placement in a social work agency. This book is concerned with how students and practice teachers can work together to maximise the student's learning during placements. The placement has many unique features as a context for learning, foremost among them:

- access to people who use social work services, who can help the student learn about good practice
- highly individualised learning opportunities, because many practice teachers have only one student at any time

Learning for a student on placement does not just happen by osmosis; it requires effort and planning by both student and practice teacher.

Placement

This refers to the period of learning during which a student is placed in a social work agency – this is sometimes referred to as the practicum. The use of the word 'practicum' is more usual in a North American context where the word 'placement' more usually refers to a child's stay with substitute carers.

Practice teacher

This term is used to describe the person in an agency who has responsibility for enabling the learning of a student. This has been used in preference to other terms because it is grounded in ideas of teaching. It does not refer to the person in the academic setting who teaches practice. Other terms are used elsewhere, for example 'field instructor' in North America.

Time spent on placement is very precious, and is remembered long after many other aspects of social work courses are forgotten. Davies (1984b), in a survey of social workers, three years after completing their professional education, found that they viewed the placement as the most enjoyable part of the course. Also, placements were seen as the best-taught components and the most useful elements of social work courses. Since Davies conducted his survey, many major changes (for example, increased legislative complexity; the acquisition of new responsibilities by social workers; new approaches to practice that challenge traditional ideologies; radical restructuring of social work education; enhancing the importance of practice learning, such as the development of competency-based approaches to learning and assessment[1]) have dramatically altered the nature of social work practice and education. These changes increase the difficulties for practice teachers and students to ensure high quality practice learning on placement. However, students' enthusiasm for placements can be maximised by methods of learning that promote effective skill development and the acquisition of skills and knowledge for social work practice. Through a variety of learning methods a range of different experiences can be generated on placement. These need to be harnessed and used actively, as Boud, Cohen and Walker suggest:

> experience is a meaningful encounter. It is not just an observation, a passive undergoing of something, but an active engagement with the environment. (Boud *et al.*, 1993, p. 6)

This is the challenge for practice teachers and students who together have to work to create a series of learning experiences on placement that engage students and promote their learning.

Practice learning

This term is used to refer to the learning that occurs whilst a student is on placement in a social work agency. It should not be taken to imply that students do not learn about practice in class settings. It refers to the context of learning in the *practice* agency.

---

1. The 'competency-based approach' to social work education has become very important in the United Kingdom. This approach specifies the detailed skills or competencies that a student must demonstrate to be competent to practise as a social worker. These competencies are the dominant force in shaping students' learning.

Learning about how to *practise* social work ought to occur throughout all sections of any course of education and training leading to a professional qualification in social work. The skills, knowledge and values of social work are not learned only in one element of the course – the placement. At different times, the placement has been seen to serve various educational functions, for example, as the time for the student to 'apply' what has been learned in class settings or as an opportunity to 'integrate theory and practice'. As Parsloe (1983) suggests, some regard the practice teacher as having the responsibility to ensure that students achieve these mystical processes. There need be nothing mysterious about a placement. It provides a complementary context to class-based learning: when taken together, class and placement learning have, by custom and experience, proved to be an effective method of promoting learning about social work practice. These two contexts for learning about social work practice, class and placement, need to be integrated, complementary, and mutually consistent. The struggle for practice teacher and student is to turn these ideals into reality.

In recent years there has been a series of major changes in practice learning. There has been a shift in emphasis in the nature of the practice teacher's role. Recently, *teaching* (through the use of a variety of teaching methods) has become a more important component of the practice teacher role. This contrasts with previous approaches where students' work was only *supervised*. Sawdon makes the observation that:

> Practice teaching used to be called student supervision. The new term aims to reflect the positive educational and training responsibilities of the practitioner who chooses to work with students. (1986, p. vii)

He stresses the notion of teaching and emphasises the duty of the practice teacher to promote learning. This is symbolised by the very title 'practice teacher'. This may be contrasted with an earlier notion of supervision; for example, Pettes stated:

Supervision is a process by which one social work practitioner enables another social work practitioner who is accountable to him to practise to the best of his ability. (1979, p. 3)

She located supervision within a managerial framework, but indicated that the function of the relationship was to promote and ensure good practice. Also in other ways, the role of the practice teacher has become modified; for example, no longer is the individual practice teacher automatically expected to provide all of the teaching for a student on placement. Often, there is involvement of the practice teacher's colleagues in the student's learning experiences. Hence, the practice teacher becomes a co-ordinator of the student's learning, rather than just a provider of learning.

There have also been major developments in social work education that have affected practice learning. In the United Kingdom there has been a greater involvement of social work agencies in social work education. This has occurred through the national requirement that social work education can only be provided by partnerships that include at least one educational institution and one social work agency. This has provided many opportunities for practice teachers to become involved in the planning of all aspects of social work education. It greatly enhances the role and function of the practice teacher and provides increased opportunities for the integration of class-based and practice-based learning. Another change of fundamental importance has been the development of competency-based approaches to social work education. These tend to specify the requirements expected of students, as a list of competencies in certain skills, that must be achieved at the end of a placement. This increase in precision is to be welcomed and helps the practice teacher determine what is required of students on placement. The model presented in this book is consistent with these approaches, though it may also be used where a competency-based approach is less strongly applied.

Key assumptions

Any book is grounded in a range of assumptions which shape both the content and the nature of discussion: often these assumptions are not made explicit and are left for the reader to discern. We wish to outline some of the key principles underlying this book, so that both the validity of the arguments and the value of the fundamental principles may be more easily judged:

Assumption one

Teaching and learning are not synonymous terms: they refer to two distinct but related activities.

Good teaching and high quality learning are inextricably linked. However, there is a very clear distinction between the activities performed by the teacher, as part of the process of seeking to promote learning, and the experiences of the learner. Whatever the intention of the teacher, it is the extent and quality of learning by the student that is important. To maximise this quality of learning, learners must be actively involved in their own learning. Hence, practice teachers must avoid a possible temptation to focus upon themselves and the activity of teaching. Similarly, learners must recognise their responsibility and not expect teachers to take responsibility for all aspects of their learning. So, high quality learning can only be achieved if both student and practice teacher work together to promote and enable learning.

Assumption two

All learners are different from each other.

All students who approach learning on placement have a wealth of past experiences of learning. Their views of learning and beliefs about what they can achieve are shaped by these previous experiences and their unique personal biography of being: black, white; female, male; gay, straight; and so on. These attributes and experiences will influence the way learning on placement is conceptualised and approached by students. Differences between learners on placement can be recognised and celebrated, because diversity and difference are not sources of problems and difficulties, but part of the backcloth to learning. Any approach to learning will only be successful to the extent that difference is not merely tolerated but actively welcomed and incorporated centrally in the processes of learning.

The structured learning model

The book presents a model of practice learning, the *structured learning model*. This model both systematises some aspects of current good practice as demonstrated on placement, and also introduces some ideas about how to create new approaches to particular aspects of the process of learning that occurs on placement. Therefore, the model is grounded and located in current approaches to practice learning but seeks to offer new perspectives. There is a series of common issues that confront all practice teachers and students, issues such as what to learn about; how to learn; how to decide if the student has reached the required level of competence. Answers to some of these questions may be prescribed by the course. Nonetheless, there will be much for the practice teacher and student to interpret and fit to their particular placement. The structured learning model suggests how some of these issues might be approached. It contains the following key elements:

- a recognition that social work is practised within societies riven by various forms of socially structured difference, for example, 'race', gender, age; and that this context of difference will significantly influence the way that practice learning occurs

- a belief that practice learning must be firmly grounded on principles derived from educational, social and psychological theories about how people learn; it is incumbent upon students and practice teachers to draw upon such theories to inform the processes of learning that occur on placement
- choices must be made about what students should learn on placement; this model introduces the idea of a practice curriculum which specifies and makes explicit those aspects of practice that a student will learn during a placement. The practice curriculum can help to formalise and guide the processes of learning on placement
- it is important that a wide variety of learning methods are used during a placement to provide a stimulating environment for the student; choices about which methods of learning to use at any particular time can be made according to a series of guiding principles
- clear, predefined standards for the examination of practice competence are needed in conjunction with a systematic approach to the collection of evidence about a student's practice abilities

All of these elements can be united and integrated through the structured learning model. This model is designed to provide practical help for practice teachers and makes explicit the processes of practice learning for students.

Overview of the book

The book is divided into two parts. In the first part, the *contexts* for practice learning are discussed. These are assumed to be common for all approaches to practice learning. In the second part of the book, a model of practice learning, the *structured learning model*, is described, and how this model can be used to promote learning is explored. Brief details of each chapter are given below.

Part I   Contexts

Chapter 1   Beginnings . . .
This chapter provides a brief overview of the book, and an introduction to some of the key assumptions that underpin the approach we have taken to practice learning.

Chapter 2   The Context of Practice Learning: The Recognition and Celebration of Difference
The social context of practice learning is considered. In particular, there is an examination of the implications for practice learning which arise in a society that is divided by *socially structured difference.* These divisions occur along several dimensions: age, disability, gender, 'race', class, and so on. Such factors influence practice learning in a variety of ways: through the relationships between students and practice teachers; the nature of the practice teacher's work; the organisational structure and culture of social work agencies; and in the nature of social work practice that the students must learn. Recognition of these issues is central to the development of high quality practice learning.

Part II   A Model for Practice Learning

Chapter 3   Theories and Models of Practice Learning
This chapter marks the second part of the book, where the emphasis shifts from examining contexts for practice learning, to the elaboration of a model of practice learning – the *structured learning model.* Other models of practice learning are reviewed, as a preliminary to discussion of the structured learning model.

Chapter 4   Understanding Learning
In this chapter some major approaches to learning are considered. A first aspect of the structured learning model is explored, that is the need to locate the model within a framework of learning theory. Without a good understanding of the principles of learning, it is impossible for students and practice teachers to construct an adequate programme of learning on placement.

Chapter 5   Using a Curriculum for Practice Learning
A curriculum for practice learning is at the heart of the structured learning model. In this chapter, the ideas implicit in this notion of a practice curriculum are considered. It is suggested that students need a clear and explicit curriculum to maximise their learning. There are difficulties in developing and using a practice curriculum, and these are recognised, considered and explored.

Chapter 6   Methods of Learning
Different methods of learning to enable students to develop practice skills, knowledge and values are examined. Methods of teaching and learning need to be diverse to maintain and sustain the interest of the learner. In the structured learning model, there are principles to help practice teachers and students choose the methods of learning to use in given situations.

Chapter 7   Examining Practice Competence
Measuring the level of attainment reached through any process of learning is difficult: it is not usually a comfortable process for the learner. However, the level of practice competence achieved by social work students must be examined at the conclusion of a programme of practice learning. The difficulties and dilemmas of making judgements about students' practice competence are explored with some suggestions about how the examination of practice can be conducted.

Chapter 8   Difficulties with Learning
There are many difficulties that may confront students in their attempts to learn while on placement. A particular difficulty facing many students is the transition to learning on placement, as opposed to learning in class situations or from not being in a formal learning environment. This transitional difficulty is considered. To help resolve this and other difficulties with learning a strategic approach is suggested.

Chapter 9   . . . Endings
The final chapter provides an approach to synthesising the various elements of the structured learning model.

2

The Context of Practice Learning: The Recognition and Celebration of Difference

Summary

All societies experience some form of socially structured difference. This common factor provides a context for the construction of practice learning. In different societies, there will be many responses to this common context that will influence the nature of practice learning. In this chapter it is argued that practice teachers and students need to recognise the existence of socially structured difference and to examine its implications for their placements. A framework to help students and practice teachers to conceptualise the impact of socially structured difference on placements is suggested. This can be used by practice teachers and students to frame their own response to fit the particular placement.

Socially structured difference

Despite differences in ideology, political belief, religion and social work practice across different societies, there is, perhaps, one irreducible element of practice learning that is of paramount importance in all cultures that practice social work. All societies experience some forms of socially structured difference, and this has implications for learning about social work on placement. The notion of socially structured difference and its implications for practice learning are complex sets of ideas and are not easily stated concisely. Nonetheless we will attempt to define socially structured difference and explore some of the implications for practice learning.

The concept of socially structured difference rests on three key elements:

- that in all societies there are different groups
- these different groups have different life chances and unequal access to the scarce resources in that society
- the inequalities between groups are determined and maintained by the powerful groups in that society. These groups exercise power over social structures to enforce social divisions: that is, the inequalities are socially determined

These elements are briefly illustrated. It is a truism to state that society consists of many different social groupings. Individuals may be classified, by others or themselves, as belonging to such categories as male/female, black/white, disabled/able-bodied, gay/straight, and so on. Often these groupings are dichotomous, but that need not imply that all individuals will always automatically be in one group or another. Individuals may be ascribed membership of different groups over time or in differing contexts. Other non-dichotomous groupings exist, such as nationality (for example, British, Chinese, French, Zambian) or religion (atheist, Buddhist, Christian, Muslim, and so on). For the individual, life chances and experiences will be influenced by ascribed membership of these social groups. It is well-documented that discrimination and oppression are experienced by those members of society who happen to be black, female, homosexual and so on (Norman, 1985; Ahmad, 1990; Biggs, 1990). These facts are well-understood and widely accepted. In any society, whatever the predominant forms of social stratification, all individuals will always have a particular and unique biography, and as a consequence will be ascribed membership of several social groupings. Therefore their life experiences will be a complex amalgam, drawing upon the discrimination or privilege that accrues to the groups to which they belong. This is well-illustrated in the work of Devore and Schlesinger who develop the concept of *ethclass* – to explain the nature of individual experience through the interaction of class and ethnicity (1991, p. 20). These ideas about the interaction of different social forces and their impact upon social groups are complex and controversial.

In constructing models of practice learning, such social realities need acknowledgement through recognition that social work is grounded in a society based upon social stratification and difference. The implications for practice learning can then be fully considered and discussed even if the precise form and character of stratification varies from society to society and over time.

Different ways of conceptualising the phenomenon of socially stratified difference exist. In the UK at present there is a growing acceptance, in social work, that the different life experiences of various social groups can only be understood as the result of structural inequalities within society. These inequalities are expressed through the operation of racism, sexism, homophobia and so on. This understanding of the nature of society is not uncontested, but it does find expression within the current paradigms operating in social work education: that is, that social work students should be enabled to deal with forces both at the individual and the structural level (CCETSW, 1991b). Terms such as 'anti-discriminatory' or 'anti-oppressive' practice are used to define this approach to social work practice although neither has a precise and universally accepted meaning. Hence it is easy to become enmeshed in debates about the precise meanings and virtues of anti-discriminatory as opposed to anti-oppressive practice; but without clear widely accepted definitions of either, fruitful dialogue about the merits of each is not easy. A feature of this arena of debate is the frequency of change in terminology or conceptualisation, and the national specivity of concepts and language. This is well-illustrated by comparing the UK and the USA. In the UK the dominant mode of conceptualisation revolves around a notion of anti-discriminatory/anti-oppressive practice while in the USA practitioners develop skills in 'cultural competence' (a little-known concept in the UK). According to Cross and colleagues, cultural competence is defined as:

> a set of congruent behaviors, attitudes, and policies that come together in a system, agency, or amongst professionals and enables that system, agency, or those professionals to work effectively in cross-cultural situations. The word culture is used because it implies the integrated pattern of human behavior that includes thoughts, communications, actions, customs, beliefs, values and institutions of a racial, ethnic, religious, or social group. (1989, p. iv)

In whatever way issues of socially structured difference are labelled and conceptualised, their existence is palpable and incontrovertible. They must be recognised in all approaches to practice learning. At least four dimensions of socially structured difference are important to consider in relation to practice learning (Shardlow and Doel, 1992b).

Learner and teacher relationships

Power is an inescapable part of the dynamic of relationships between all teachers and students. This is especially true where the teacher has considerable influence on decisions about the student's level of competence. Practice learning presents an extreme case, because the practice teacher often provides the majority of teaching on placement and may be then a key arbiter in the decision to pass or fail a student. It is, therefore, highly likely that students will feel some apprehension by virtue of the role they occupy and the nature of their relationship to practice teachers. Performance of tasks by some students may be adversely affected by this apprehension. Making mistakes, and being open about these, can be more difficult with a teacher who occupies a position of such power and who has so much influence on judgements about students' practice competence (Pettes, 1967). In the past, insufficient attention has been paid to the nature of this relationship and to how it is experienced by students and teachers; only by emphasizing the importance of this relationship can high quality practice learning be achieved.

We will now consider some of the implications of this aspect of the practice teacher/student relationship. Both practice teacher and student will have an individual biography and will have affiliation to various social groups: male/female, black/white, disabled/able-bodied, gay/straight, and so on. The relationship between teacher and student will be mediated through the personal experiences of both individuals. The relationship of two women, as teacher and student, will be different in its nature to the relationship between a male practice teacher and a female student. In the latter example, their respective experiences of being male and being female will influence how the relationship between those individuals as teacher/learner or examiner/candidate is experienced.

Illustrative example

If the student is female, and sees herself as being:

- less powerful in social transactions than men
- discriminated against by social structures
- denied access to social commodities by virtue of being female

then she may experience the learning relationship as reinforcing those patterns – *if she has a male practice teacher*. As a consequence, she may be unable to express herself fully through her social work practice, and may become excessively conformist or excessively

> confrontational. The distribution of power within the practice teacher/student relationship may replicate the allocation of power between the student and the world of men, external to the learning on placement.

It is the responsibility of the practice teacher to create opportunities and structures which minimise the likelihood of placement failure or poor performance on placement resulting from socially structured differences between practice teachers and students. There are at least three ways to create these opportunities.

Recognise difference

At the beginning of a placement, the practice teacher has a responsibility to introduce discussion about socially structured difference. Most students, at this stage of the placement, will be a little nervous and likely to regard the practice teacher as a powerful person who has influence over the shape of their placement. This may result in the student being reluctant to introduce sensitive issues into the discussion. The act of instigating debate is an acknowledgement by the practice teacher of the existence of social diversity and, importantly, gives permission to the student to discuss personal aspects of socially structured differences. If the practice teacher is reluctant to talk about social diversity, such feelings and attitudes will be evident to the student. Only by positive espousal of those issues, through lack of fear about the content and nature of discussion, can socially structured differences in the practice teacher/student relationship be validated. Through such approaches, a positive climate for considering socially structured difference can be generated. Discussion about socially structured difference by members of dominant social groups can concentrate on the negative experiences of some groups. This tendency to focus on negative aspects of difference can reinforce negative stereotypes of some groups, allowing us to forget that diversity is a source of richness. Diversity is a cause for celebration and positive aspects of difference *must* be considered, as well as the negative, in the practice teacher/student relationship. Moving beyond simple acknowledgement, through validation, to celebration is a core task for student and practice teacher. Early discussion can only be the first step, not a resolution.

It is easy when discussing socially structured difference to use rather grand, if somewhat general, terms such as identify, recognise, and celebrate – without stating the precise practice implications of these words. What can the student expect that the practice teacher might do to help deal with some of these issues in the practice learning environment? At the first meeting between practice teacher and student, there must be some discussion about socially structured difference and how this will influence the place-ment. In the early practice tutorials, the student must be given the opportunity to explore personal feelings about the configuration of socially structured difference within the practice teacher/student duo. Similarly, practice teachers must be open and discuss their views about these issues.

Practice tutorials or tutorials

These terms are used to describe the face-to-face teach-ing sessions between practice teacher and student – the ward 'tutorials' avoids the connotations of 'super-vision', and the inelegant 'practice teaching session.'

The purpose of these discussions is to inquire into the effects of social structured difference upon personal in-teraction, placement processes and, most importantly, ways in which learning might be influenced. If the practice teacher belongs to a group which might often be seen to be dominant, careful consideration must be given to mech-anisms used to raise these issues. Simple questions asked by practice teachers in dialogue may elicit bland responses from some students, through lack of trust that their concerns will be heard and acted on. Trust cannot be established solely through the acknowledgement of feelings of oppression, but depends upon the creation of an open climate for learning, where issues can be addressed. Discussions about socially structured difference and its impact on the learning environment need to continue throughout the placement, as a mechanism to ensure the promotion of learning. It is the practice teacher's responsibility to direct attention towards this aspect of learning.

It is also important to recognise any potential limitations to the learning environment deriving from the type and quality of experience contained within the practice teacher/ student duo. For example, if both are white there will be a lack of black perspectives within the tutorial structure. Similarly, if both are male, there will be an absence of female perspectives. Ways need to be sought to remedy these deficits through the range of experience and opportunities available during the placement either by mechanisms such as the use of external consultants (see below) or attention to the type of work undertaken.

Reference groups

It is not desirable for the relationship between student and practice teacher to exclude others who might contribute to the process of students' learning. Students may benefit from the opportunity to participate in reference groups consisting of other staff who belong to the same or similar, self-defined, socially structured group as the student. Such groups can provide a sense of validation for students' perspectives where this could not be sufficiently achieved within the confines of the practice teacher/student duo. No criticism is implied of either student or practice teacher if a student wishes to participate in a reference group. Consideration must be given by both the practice teacher and student to the amount of time spent in such group activities and also the range and scope of the group. If groups discuss actions that students ought to pursue, there may be a potential for conflict with the advice given by practice teachers. Sensitively handled, these differences in opinion create fertile soil for learning. Through exploration of these differences, greater understandings are generated through a synthesis derived from the practice teacher's, student's and group approaches. Involvement in reference groups may occur in other ways, for example, client-based organisations and groups. Students can achieve self-validation for their perspective through direct action with clients from the same social group.

External consultants

Where the practice teacher/student duo does not provide sufficient opportunity for the student's self-validation within a given perspective, it may be beneficial for an external consultant to become involved. This can compensate for these deficits by providing the missing opportunities for discussion and debate within the orbit of a particular perspective, allowing students the experience of discussing social work practice using common and shared concepts, similar personal histories and the (probable) common experiences of oppression. Some of the difficulties identified with reference groups may be even more apparent with an external consultant. Strong emotional bonds may develop between student and consultant and advice given by external consultants may differ from that given by practice teachers. These potential difficulties need to be foreseen and a detailed written agreement can help to reduce the risk of misunderstandings.

Agency structure and policy

The second major dimension of socially structured difference that affects learning on placement is the agency's structure and policy. In social work agencies, a *climate* for practice is generated by policies adopted, operation of managerial styles, and organisational profile – factors such as flow of information, nature of hierarchy, patterns of meetings and so on. Practice teachers need to be able to recognise, describe and characterise this climate, to be able to register changes in temperature or pressure in particular zones of the organisation. This helps them to guide students to locations where innovative practice may be undertaken without too much risk. The ability of practice teachers to know about the agency climate will, in reality, be limited by their position in the organisation. It may be quite difficult to develop a broad vision of the agency climate for practice.

It is to be expected that any agency will have policies and structures that are more affirming to some groups experiencing oppression than others. For example, there may be extensive policies about sexual harassment, but few ensuring women are given equal opportunities at the point of recruitment or promotion. Or there may be distinct differences between the range and scope of policies promoting the rights of black people, and relatively few of direct relevance to those with disability. Similarly, the agency may, through each of these elements, manifest a greater concern with the rights of employees than of clients or vice versa. To understand this climate a range of indicators are available to students and practice teachers. Some of the more important are:

- the extent of active involvement by external groups in the provision of advice and policy formulation
- the existence and nature of internal support groups and reference groups for staff experiencing oppression
- the easy availability of policy documents
- the adequacy of structures which monitor the effectiveness of policy implementation, especially the effects upon those experiencing oppression
- the existence of agency employment profiles indicating the number and distribution of men and women, black and white people, and so on, in the organisation and the existence of effective policies to ensure fairness in employment practices

Practice teachers need to enable social work students to learn the skills of reading the agency climate through using these and other similar indicators, so that students are equipped to function effectively within any given climate.

Content of social work practice

The third important dimension of socially structured difference is concerned with the nature of social work practice, and in particular with the practice teacher's own work.
Students are expected to possess knowledge, skills and
values which demonstrate an ability to work anti-oppressively
(CCETSW, 1989). Regrettably for students and practitioners,
there is no clear exposition of what is to be understood
by this requirement. It would be most unjust if students
were expected to define for the rest of the profession,
through their practice, the nature and content of anti-
oppressive practice. Social work has yet to translate the
concept of anti-oppressive practice into a set of recognisable
features which can be readily put into practice. Individual
practice teachers need to come to some understanding
about how they conceptualise this aspect of practice, and
how they intend to promote students' abilities to practise
anti-oppressively. This is not the place to develop an extended discussion about the nature of anti-oppressive
practice itself. Attempting a grand theoretical overview
might in any case be a mistaken enterprise at present. A
more fruitful mechanism might be to begin to define anti-
oppressive practice through some of the constituent parts
of such a practice, looking initially, for example, at issues
of 'race', gender, disability, age and so on. Then, from
good practice in these separate components of oppression,
it may be possible to construct a synthesis, revealing a
grand theory of anti-oppressive practice.

Such a current theoretical vacuum leaves the practice
teacher in a difficult position. At first sight practice teachers
and students might seem to be on their own in having to
develop individualised approaches to anti-oppressive practice. However there is cause for considerable optimism
in this field, and there are a number of recent publications that have provided helpful materials for practice
teachers and students to develop an anti-oppressive approach to practice learning (CCETSW, 1991a; Humphries,
et al., 1993; ILPS, 1993; Thompson, 1993). It is therefore
incumbent on all practice teachers to use those materials

that are available to help define and develop their own approach to anti-oppressive/anti-discriminatory practice in a meaningful way. Then and only then will they be in a position to convey to students the nature of the content of anti-oppressive/anti-discriminatory practice.

Curriculum

The final dimension of socially structured difference focuses upon what the student learns whilst on placement: the *content* of learning. This is often referred to as the curriculum that a student follows. Those unfamiliar with the notion of a curriculum, or its application to practice learning, may need to read Chapter 5 before reading this section. Incorporating a systematic approach to socially structured difference within the curriculum can be a perplexing task for practice teachers and students. Two models, *integrated* and *permeated*, have been identified by Ahmed, specifically addressing 'race' (Ahmed, 1987). Similar ideas have been proposed in relation to gender: Phillipson, using a sewing metaphor, suggests there are two types of curriculum, patchwork models (integrated) and woven-thread models (permeated) (Phillipson, 1992). The elements of these two types of curriculum are as follows.

Integration model

In this model there are discrete elements of learning that treat aspects of socially structured difference (for example, 'race', gender, sexuality) as separate items for discussion. These elements of the curriculum may be of any size, according to how the curriculum is constructed. This type of approach is best illustrated by an example. Suppose a practice curriculum contained a unit of learning entitled 'professional orientation'. This unit might include some of the following areas for a student to learn on placement:

- joining an agency, and getting to know the staff and structures
- understanding yourself in relation to professional ethics
- how to manage and structure your time
- 'race' and professional practice

Thus this curriculum has a *separate* element about 'race'. There might also be other separate parts of the curriculum about other forms of oppression such as gender issues.

Permeation model

In the permeation model socially structured difference permeates all parts of the practice curriculum – so that it is impossible to consider any aspect of learning without examining socially structured difference. For example 'race' and gender are not separate elements within a particular part of the curriculum. Rather they are central to, and indivisible from, all parts of the curriculum. Again, an example may help to illustrate this approach. Suppose a part of the practice curriculum included a section about the preparation of reports for the court. Instead of considering initially items such as court policy, agency guidelines, or interviewing practices, this segment of learning might begin with an analysis of the ways in which those who experience oppression are served by the reports that are prepared for the court. This might reveal that black people are more likely than white people to be given a custodial sentence for equivalent offences. This insight can then be used as a springboard for developing ideas about good practice. In the permeation model all the parts of the curriculum would centrally include discussion of socially structured difference.

Ahmed is severely critical of the integration model. According to her view, it may give the impression that the experiences of black people and other ethnic minorities are of marginal importance, and therefore they can be treated as an adjunct to the main curriculum (similar arguments can be made in relation to other groups who experience oppression). By contrast she strongly favours the permeation model and argues that in relation to 'race':

> the permeation model is about suffusing all the teaching with anti-racism in a fundamental and radical way: an anti-racism which is informed by a progressive black perspective – one which commits itself wholeheartedly to the promotion of black communities' interests. (1987, p. ii)

Her rejection of the integration model is severe. However, it need not be rejected absolutely, as the integrated model may represent a transitional first step to the development of a curriculum that fully addresses socially structured difference. A practice teacher who has devised and used some discrete sections of curriculum about socially structured difference with students may be able to develop from these a curriculum that employs the permeation model. This need not be the case for all teachers; some may wish to move straight to an integrated model. Intermediate models may be developed which incorporate permeated models in some units of the curriculum linked to integrated elements in other units.

Whichever model is selected, the act of adopting a curriculum-based approach (where the content of learning is made explicit) eases the tasks for the practice teacher of incorporating material about socially structured difference. First, it permits monitoring of the amount of time spent by the student on these issues. Conventional wisdom suggests that in the past many students, although not all, have spent insufficient time engaging with these issues. Second, where the learning opportunities presented on placement are not providing sufficient range or quality of learning, then the practice teacher can introduce other material to compensate for this deficiency in the placement experience. This type of problem most usually arises on placements where the ethnicity of the client population is regarded as insufficiently diverse to meet the student's learning needs (so-called 'white areas'). Finally, in this area of practice, many students feel highly challenged and personally insecure; making explicit learning requirements can help allay these fears.

Celebrating difference

Students belonging to powerful groups within society may need to think carefully about themselves and their social origins. Some may take the erroneous view that only those from minorities[1] need to consider issues of socially structured difference. Students from minorities tend, by virtue of their daily experience, to be sensitised to issues of difference – but not always. It must be a responsibility of the practice teacher to ensure that *all* students on placement carefully consider this area of practice, to ensure that all students develop the knowledge, skills and values necessary to practice social work in a society based upon socially structured difference. To achieve this end practice teachers and students need to work together, to seek and use positive and creative examples of diversity that genuinely bring varied and diverse perspectives to the practice arena. This entails using the strengths of different cultural, social, racial, and religious groups to bring new and creative insights into social work practice.

The example overleaf demonstrates the possibility of using different approaches to social problems, approaches that are grounded in a variety of different traditions. When introduced into learning about social work they enrich practice and give cause to celebrate diversity.

---

1. It is not usual in the UK to use the term 'minority' as a collective adjective to refer to all students, black, gay, female, etc. who may experience oppression. Part of the reason may be that women are not a minority within the population for the UK. We have adopted the US terminology in part because there is no such collective term in the UK, partially because it expresses minority status in terms of the distribution of power, where certain groups do not receive a fair share of society's various resources. However, we recognise that the term 'minority' has its problems.

Illustrative example

Whanau is the Maori word for family. In New Zealand, Maori ideas about the working and ways of families have influenced the way in which social work professionals, Maori and pakeha (white), work with both Moari and pakeha to help families to make decisions at points of crisis. Building upon traditional Maori family group meetings, involving many family members coming together, social workers are enabling families to liberate their resources (Doel and Shardlow, 1993).

Part II

A Model for Practice Learning

... an exploration of the elements of a particular model of practice learning: the structured learning model

3

Theories and Models of Practice Learning

Summary

This chapter provides a brief definition of a 'theory' and a 'model' before describing the extent to which theory is incorporated into writing about practice learning. Several different models of practice learning are described. Finally, a brief outline of the structured learning model – the model advocated in this book – is presented.

Theory, models and approaches

There are a variety of different models, theories and approaches to practice learning. Some purport to help the practice teacher and student with practical advice about what to do on placement. Others offer more conceptual advice about the nature of learning or the organisation of placements. Before exploring some of these theories, models and approaches, it is necessary to consider the nature of these three concepts.

Theories represent an attempt to bring order and regularity into our experience. A key characteristic of a theory is that it provides an explanation about a given phenomenon. A succinct definition of the nature of theory is given by Howe:

a theory may now be defined as a set of concepts and propositions that present an organised view of phenomena. By proposing order and pointing out relationships, theories enable their users to do four important things as they set about their particular bit of the world:

1   To describe.
2   To explain.
3   To predict.
4   To control and bring about. (1987, p. 12)

Howe's definition identifies what a theory ought to contain and illustrates the kind of use that can be made of theory. The explanation offered by any particular theory is supposed to be general and widely applicable. Moreover, the type of theory often associated with the natural sciences assumes that a theory is valid as an explanation of a given phenomenon if it is empirically testable and falsifiable. These notions of theory are controversial: for example, post-modernist thinking repudiates the plausibility of grand theories which purport to offer large-scale explanations (Boyne and Rattansi, 1990). Instead, small-scale theorising is preferred, building upon the unique experience of individuals to incorporate different realities. This post-modernist view of theory is very different to the traditional account of theory. A substantial body of literature on the nature of theory and social explanation exists. For present purposes, there is no necessity to argue for any particular view of the nature of theory. In the context of practice learning, theory can be taken to be of two distinct types:

- theories about the nature, function and purpose of practice learning
- theories that describe how to promote students' learning on placement – with an explanation of why the theory is effective. These theories are most usually drawn from other disciplines, for example, psychological and sociological theories about how adults learn

There are few examples of theories *about* practice learning, but there have been significant attempts to incorporate theory from other disciplines to inform the work of practice teachers.

Models offer a description rather than an explanation. They are less comprehensive than theories, but are designed to offer guidance about ways of behaving in given sets of circumstances, Payne states:

> *models* – describing what happens during practice in a general way, applying to a wide range of situations, in a structured way, so that they extract certain principles and patterns of activity that give the practice consistency. (1991, p. 50)

This notion of a model is perhaps less controversial than the differing accounts of theory. Possibly the most important feature of any model is that it is useful. A good model will suggest actions that might be chosen from a range of different possibilities. A model should be capable of being used by different people in different contexts. For the practice teacher and student a model of practice learning is one that offers suggestions about how to go about the various types of activity that are part of a student's learning on placement.

There are a variety of different models of practice learning; some of these incorporate theoretical concepts from other disciplines to inform the actions of practice teachers and students.

Approaches, as Payne suggests, are a way of individuals ordering their minds about particular issues or problems (1991). So that, to have a particular approach may be helpful in performing a given task. An approach does not necessarily suggest any particular explanation or justification for the way an individual behaves. If there are no explanatory theories or models available to indicate possible courses of action then it may be useful to have a constant approach. Practice teachers and students may choose, on placement, to share and develop a joint approach to some aspects of practice learning.

An approach is unique to one or perhaps a few people and less precisely conceptualised than models and theories, so we will confine our attention to published models and theories.

At different times during the placement, practice teachers and students will probably need to draw on a range of theories, models and approaches to inform the development of practice learning in their particular context. To help with this process some key writings in the field of practice learning will be examined.

Theory and practice learning

There is not a great deal of writing about practice learning, and only in recent years has the subject area attracted discussion, debate and theorising. This growing interest has been fostered by the recognition that only through high quality practice learning can students achieve high quality practice with clients. Despite the modest amount of published material, it will not all be comprehensively reviewed here; rather the intention is to demonstrate current theorising about practice learning by selecting some representative examples of recent literature. To do this, a fourfold classification of materials is used to illustrate the range of current theorising.

1. Practical literature

One major and very important strand of writing about practice learning can be termed *practical*. In this type of literature, there is a very strong emphasis upon offering advice about a variety of practical aspects of practice learning. Discussions of the theoretical underpinnings of practice learning are not strongly present or may be absent altogether. Danbury's book, *Teaching Practical Social Work* (1986), provides a recent example of this trend. The book begins with some general considerations about 'expectations of departments', 'objectives of a CQSW[1] course', 'expectations of local authority students', 'college days and place-

---

1. CQSW: the Certificate of Qualification in Social Work, a professional qualification in social work, now superseded by the Diploma in Social Work.

ment days', 'concurrent vs block placements', 'agency meetings' and the 'length of placements'. The remainder of the book is dominated by similar practical concerns such as recording, selecting cases, and the evaluation of placement aims. Throughout the book the reader is provided with a series of suggestions for good practice, of which the following extracts are typical:

> Whenever possible the supervisor and student should meet before the start of the placement, with or without the tutor. (p. 11)

> The student will need to know if or when the supervisor is available outside the set supervision time, for advice or consultation. (p. 21)

> It is helpful for both the supervisor and the student to keep notes on the supervisory sessions. (p. 71)

This book and similar types of literature represent the need for practice teachers and students to have some guidelines about what to do on placement. It does not offer an analysis of theoretical underpinnings of practice learning. Nor does it seek to develop theories about the nature of practice learning. The function of this type of literature is not to engage in theory-building but to offer advice. In the practical literature, aspects of theory are often implicit rather than made explicit. This can be a disadvantage as it may lead some practice teachers and students to assume that only the practical is important, or that there is no need for theory-building in the field of practice learning.

2. Located literature

In the *located* strand of literature about practice learning, authors explicitly identify the theoretical underpinning that supports their writing. This contributes to the development of theoretical debate about the nature of practice learning. Located materials may not have substantial discussion about theory, but they do make explicit the theories that support and contribute to their writing. Thompson, Osada and Anderson's book, *Practice Teaching in Social Work* (1990), begins with a very brief, but important, discussion of patterns of adult learning. This forms a theoretical basis for subsequent practical guidance about how to promote learning on placement through discussion of areas such as pre-placement planning, selection of workload, the supervisory process, and so on. This brief extract on 'supervision' illustrates their use of theory:

> Practice teachers need to be clear what supervision means, in theory and reality. We all tend to carry around some notion of supervision in practice, and often this is informed by bad or poor personal experience of being supervised. However, whether a student or an experienced social work practitioner, there is nothing as valuable or energising as 'good' supervision. But what is good supervision; how is it achieved? We will consider this, by reviewing the content of student supervision and its process as these are key aspects of effective practice teaching. (p. 35)

In this extract the authors state the need to understand supervision in a theoretical context and they begin to develop the possibility of different supervisory techniques, such as: giving a protected workload to students; immersing them fully in the hurly-burly of everyday practice; or learning through observing an experienced practitioner p. 35). The theoretical components form a basis from which to develop their guidelines. As the extract illustrates, the emphasis is still on the practical rather than the theoretical. This strand of writing is well-represented and a range of texts might be described as located: for example, Ford and Jones's book, *Student Supervision* (1987), has discussion of different methods of practice teaching and of theories about learning, but remains dominated by similar concerns to those of Thompson, Osada and Anderson. An interesting example of the located strand of writing about practice learning is Butler and Elliot's *Teaching and Learning for Practice* (1985). They use Jungian psychological theory as a springboard for their work.

3. Grounded literature

The *grounded* element of practice learning literature takes a particular theory or construct and uses this throughout the text, exploring the ramifications of the original theory or construct to explain and inform how to promote practice learning. An example of this type of literature is Bogo and Vayda's book *The Practice of Field Instruction in Social Work,* 1987). In the first chapter of this book, Bogo and Vayda explicitly state:

> Field instruction is a unique area of social work practice and is applied through an interactive process. We propose to describe and discuss the theoretical construct upon which field instruction is based and to develop the process of its application. (p. 1)

Anchored firmly to the idea that a theoretical stance is central to understanding practice learning, Bogo and Vayda develop what they term the 'loop model of field instruction' (see section on models). This is grounded upon a theoretical understanding about the nature of learning. However, the particular content is not relevant for our present purposes; what is significant is their recognition that practice teaching is grounded in a theoretical understanding and their explanation of that theoretical basis.

4. Analytical literature

Analytical literature represents the final aspect of our brief categorisation of the types of literature about practice learning. The analytical strand does not draw solely on theories from other disciplines as a foundation for practice learning. Rather, it is theorising *about* the activity of practice learning. One of the earliest, if not the very first, publication to identify the existence of different theoretical models of practice learning was written by Wijnberg and Schwartz (1977). They consider three different models of student supervision – apprentice, growth, and role systems; they summarise the importance of identifying different models in the following way:

The conceptualization of these models provides (1) a framework against which to compare their distinctive characteristics and their metamorphosis over time, (2) a structure in which to look at our own supervisory goals and intervention strategies, and (3) a paradigm within which to structure as well as analyze interactions. (p. 107)

They state very concisely and crisply the value of theory to practice learning, emphasising strongly the benefit of a comparative theorising.

Theory-building

As yet, there are no fully comprehensive theories of practice learning. This fact should not surprise us, since the very practical nature of the subject, coupled with the lack of substantial interest until relatively recently, has discouraged theory-building. It would be a very ambitious project to develop a theory of and for practice learning. However, there is a range of different models of very direct use and currently accessible to practice teachers and students.

Models of practice learning

There are a variety of different models of practice learning that offer a description of current practice combined with some guidance for practice teachers and students about how to enable practice learning. The major models of practice learning reviewed here do not possess equal or even similar levels of generality or content. This can make a direct comparison between the value and importance of various models difficult. Also, Wijnberg and Schwartz (1977) remind us that in thinking about models of practice learning we are thinking about 'ideal types' as described by Max Weber. An ideal type consists of a description of a concept including all the major attributes usually associated with the concept. Ideal types are useful in describing and analysing sociological phenomena. Perfect examples of these ideal types, possessing all the associated major characteristics, rarely exist in a pure form in the real world. So it is with models of practice learning. The examples described are rarely found in a pure form, but they illustrate the most important models that can be used by practice teachers and students.

The first four models of those which follow have been, or are, dominant in the UK – even if not always mentioned explicitly in the majority of published literature. These are the apprenticeship, the competency–based the growth and development, and the managerial.

The apprenticeship model

This was the original model for teaching social work students about practice, and it remains influential (Kutzik, 1977; George, 1982). In the apprenticeship model, students learn how to practice social work primarily through experience of direct work with clients. For the students, 'doing social work' enables learning social work, by providing experiences that they can reflect upon to develop their practice under the guidance of the practice teacher. Social work in this model is like a craft, with accumulated wisdom passing from one generation to another.

The primary method for promoting learning is the weekly meeting (practice tutorial)[1] between the student and the experienced practitioner. During the tutorial, as preparation for completing pieces of work, the student is given instruction about how to work by an experienced practitioner. Also during the practice tutorial, detailed scrutiny is undertaken on a case-by-case basis of work that has been completed. In this model, process recording – where students write a very detailed account of interactional exchanges between themselves and their clients – has been

---

1. There are many different names to refer to this meeting; practice teaching session, supervision session. We use the name 'practice tutorial' to emphasise the focus on learning and that only one or at the most a very small number of students are present. See the box on page 19.

heavily used as a tool to promote learning (Holden, 1972; Urdang, 1979; Wilson, 1981, p. 118; Danbury, 1986, p. 38). Contact between the social work course and the practice teacher is likely to be at a minimal level; the model incorporates an assumption that students will learn if placed with experienced practice teachers, in an agency where there is a climate conducive to good social work practice – in other words, learning by a kind of osmosis. Hence, there is no need for close joint planning of students' learning between academic institution and practice agency. No model is static, but as Wijnberg and Schwartz comment about the apprenticeship model:

> the underlying structure has remained the same: regular, private conferences with supervisors in which they can pass on their accumulated practice wisdom and instruct workers in applying this knowledge to their own caseload. (1977, p. 108)

More recently developments in the application of this model have occurred, and this can be seen in the variety of ways now available for practice teachers to demonstrate the skills of practice. Demonstration is no longer restricted to verbal instruction by the practice teacher; for example, Sheafor and Jenkins (1982) suggest that observation of experienced practitioners by students is one of the ways to enable learning. This view is expounded more forcefully by Bogo and Vayda indicating the potential benefits for the student of this mode of learning:

> Knowledge, skill, values and attitudes are transmitted to the student through observing an experienced professional at work and observing emulating, or modelling one's own behaviour on that of the field instructor. (1987, p. 20)

This model has been a dominant paradigm for practice learning in the UK in recent years. Until recently, there has been a marked reluctance on the part of many practice teachers to allow students to observe their practice, or indeed for practice teachers to observe students. There are differences of opinion about the content and nature of this model.

According to Sheafor and Jenkins (1982) the student learns, in this model, from the experiential content of working with particular case materials. From this experience the student, facilitated by the practice teacher, is able to develop general theories of practice, through induction. However, Bogo and Vayda do not regard reflection as a part of the apprenticeship model; they suggest that the apprenticeship model appears to focus on behaviour and strategies, but omits reflective and conceptual activities.

> The instructor [practice teacher] is not specifically directed to help the student become aware of how their own values and assumptions can affect their perception of phenomena and their practice intervention. Nor is the instructor directed to help the student identify and use appropriate concepts from the professional knowledge base to understand phenomena and plan responses. (1987, p. 21)

There is a danger that when practised in a busy office, this model collapses into instruction by the practice teacher on how to work with each case according to the agency's expectations.

Competency-based models

Competency-based models have found much favour in recent years in the UK, where they underpin official regulations governing professional social work education (CCETSW, 1991b; CCETSW, 1992). These models are broad in application and relate not just to the experience of students on placement but to the whole arena of social work education. Clark (1976) suggests that programmes incorporating this model have been realised in many diverse ways but that they have common characteristics such as:

- an emphasis upon the outcome of learning rather than the process of achieving learning – these models usually specify the requirements that a student must demonstrate to show that they have successfully completed a piece of learning. The methods of learning are often seen as less important than what is achieved by the student

- teaching and learning are defined in performance terms – students must be able to demonstrate that they can do certain prescribed tasks to show that they have successfully completed a piece of learning
- outcomes are stated as behavioural objectives – the requirements of students are usually given in very clear written statements that list behaviours that students must be able to perform
- the use of criteria for measuring performance – the degree to which a student is successful in achieving the required outcomes is measured through precisely stated criteria that indicate differing levels of competence

In competency-based models the starting point is, paradoxically, the end of the educational process. Hence, the attributes of a competent social worker are carefully and precisely defined in the model, in terms of the kind of behaviours required to fulfil the role of being a social worker. These behaviours are generally specified by the educational institution as a series of competencies (a competency is a carefully worded statement that describes a behavioural skill). Students must achieve certain competencies at given points in the course. There may be some flexibility for students and practice teachers to negotiate the competencies that will be achieved at the end of a period of learning. Once the competencies are clear and agreed for a placement it is for the practice teacher and student to negotiate the learning objectives that will help the student to meet the competencies. The practice teacher is, in this model, an adviser and facilitator to aid the student's learning and achievement of the competencies.

Commenting upon some of the literature about this model, Bogo and Vayda (1987) observe that most attention has been given to the use of this model either in class or in the laboratory. This is unfortunate as the model has been extensively applied to practice learning in the

UK. Bogo and Vayda summarise the model in the following terms: it

> focuses on concretising a particular professional knowledge base in the form of measurable behaviours. It appears little attention is paid to reflection, based on the student's own experience. (1987, p. 25)

Competency-based models are a very important component of practice learning in the UK, where they are very influential both in practice learning and in the construction of social work education programmes and courses.

The growth and development model

The growth and development model draws upon Freudian and neo-Freudian psychology. The essence of this model is to develop students' self-awareness as a precursor to competent practice with clients. A first step in achieving proficiency in social work practice is a recognition by the student of the importance of the relationship between the resolution of the student's personal intra-psychic conflicts and high quality professional practice. Personal 'growth', the resolution of the student's psychological problems, is achieved through this recognition and subsequent work in the practice tutorial. Without progression and 'growth', the student will not be able to help clients.

In such a model the key function of the student's practice teacher is to modify inappropriate attitudes which are part of the student's psyche. Hence, the focus for practice tutorials will be the problems experienced by the student, who will be encouraged to reveal these to the supervisor. During practice tutorials, the feelings the student has about clients will be examined in considerable detail, as the student is assumed to identify closely with clients, and to internalise, or react to, feelings engendered by clients. Through the exploration of these current feelings and attitudes juxtaposed with historic personal problems the practice teacher can help the student to achieve personal 'growth'. In these circumstances the boundary between therapy and practice teaching is thin. According to Wijnberg and Schwartz (1977), some theorists have argued that this boundary must be maintained, others that the preservation of this boundary is less important than the student's achievement of growth. In a practical sense the distinction between therapy and education cannot be easy to maintain, given the nature and content of material being discussed by student and practice teacher.

This model is highly individualised, since the nature of practice learning must of necessity be quite distinct for each student. By its nature, it is not an open model, where student and practice teacher negotiate the learning to be undertaken. The reverse is the case, because the student is regarded as a person-with-problems for which the practice teacher knows the remedy. Denial by the student of the existence of a problem becomes a defence against active engagement, and a barrier to the achievement of competent social work practice. Inevitably, students may sometimes feel undermined by practice teachers who focus on personal problems (Rosenblatt and Meyer, 1975).

Siporin argues that this model was largely rejected during the 1960s and 1970s in the USA (Bogo and Vayda, 1987, p. 22), although it has been slightly more durable in the UK.

The managerial model

The managerial model is prevalent where *good* social work is defined as current agency practice and where there is little reference to national codes of practice or other independent definitions of social work practice. These conditions prevail in many agencies in the UK, where this is the current *default* model of practice learning. A central thrust of the managerial model is the need for agencies to protect clients from poor practice and to construct models of practice learning where this imperative is dominant. In this model, the function of the practice teacher is to initiate the student into agency policy, procedure and practice. A problem-solving approach focusing on individual cases or pieces of work will frequently be employed. Pieces of work are discussed in practice tutorials, where objectives, planned actions and reviews of work done are located within the confines of agency policy and practice. This model of practice learning engenders conformity and rule-governed behaviour among students. It also promotes a view of social work practice which can be understood entirely in terms of agency practice. It is a powerful and pervasive model for learning about social work practice and in its degenerate form the managerial model is reduced to an unthinking adherence to the dominant orthodoxy prevailing in an agency.

The academic model

The central tenet of the academic model is that students need to develop their cognitive appreciation of social work before engaging in practice with clients. This principle is expressed through the organisation of curriculum and learning. Teaching in class must come before practice, which in the extreme form of this model may be a single block of practice experience after the completion of all class teaching. Modified versions exist, where a placement follows a period of class-based learning, with the specific purpose of applying learning in a given practice context. George described the early development of this model in the United States, and characterised the model as an attempt to define a more scientific notion of learning about social work, arising from a reaction to earlier 'learning by doing' models of social work (1982, p. 41).

It may be tempting to reduce the academic model to a single organisational principle that defines the order of classroom learning and practice experience, yet this would be a misrepresentation. The model is based upon assumptions about learning: for example, that competent practice is not possible without prior intellectual understanding. According to Sheafor and Jenkins this assumption can be interpreted to imply that:

the student is expected to deduce a practice approach from classroom learning. (1982, p. 15)

The model suggests that intellectual knowledge will prepare the student to perform as a social work practitioner. For the practice teacher, this model may either be a blessing or a hindrance, as students are expected to arrive on placement having been taught all they need to know. The practice teacher's role is to provide opportunities for the student to apply prior knowledge to practice and to assist students as they grapple with the interaction of their knowledge with direct practice. There is no requirement for the practice teacher to teach theory on placement. In this model, the practice teacher is not so much a teacher, more a facilitator to help the student apply theoretical learning to actual practice.

Sheafor and Jenkins identify some of the more obvious difficulties with this model:

> students may wish to try out in practice theoretical approaches concurrently with intellectual learning about those approaches; retaining information without opportunities to practice the knowledge can both be frustrating and knowledge can be lost; irrelevant material may be taught as part of the academic components of the course; practice agencies may complain about students' lack of preparedness for practice. (1982, p. 16)

A danger with this model is that the development of practice skills may seem to be of secondary importance in comparison to the acquisition of theoretical knowledge about social work.

The articulated model

The articulated model recognises the importance of academic learning about social work and learning how to practise social work. Neither form of learning is given preeminence over the other. The integration of these two forms of learning is central to this model; this is expressed at the organisational level to help encourage students to integrate academic theory and practice. According to Sheafor and Jenkins (1982), this integration is achieved through close collaboration of class-based and agency-based teachers. However, they recognise that ideal levels of collaboration are rarely achieved, because of the very high costs placed on staff; to create and maintain the planning and communication structures necessary for a full implementation of the articulated model requires considerable time and resources.

In this model, the curriculum is jointly planned by class and practice teachers. This requires careful consideration of how students can be enabled to use knowledge or experiences gained either in class or practice to further their understanding about social work. Throughout the model, the wholeness of the student's experience is stressed – Sheafor and Jenkins suggest that this can best be recognised through structures such as concurrent placements.

One of the difficulties for proponents of this model centres upon the intrinsic problems associated with integrating theory and practice. Parsloe has suggested that the 'gap' between field and practice may be somewhat more complex than is implied by a simplistic recognition of a need to bring together theory and practice. There are various structural barriers to the integration of theory and practice; for example, different sets of assumptions held by those who work in agencies and those who teach in universities act as an obstruction to full implementation of the articulated model (Parsloe, 1983). Such barriers might make the implementation of an articulated model rather more difficult than is implied just by resource constraints. Nonetheless, a major defect of the model is cost, and many programmes do not have the resources necessary to develop the articulated model.

The loop model of practice learning

From experiences of practice learning in Canada, Bogo and Vayda (1987) have constructed what they term a 'loop' model of practice learning. More than any of the other models presented so far, this is a model of learning rather than teaching. Their model suggests a mechanism to enable and make explicit practice learning and is grounded in Kolb's four-stage model of learning (Kolb, 1976), which they have adapted to develop a model of how to enable learning on placement.

This model consists of four phases: retrieval, reflection, linkage and professional response. These four phases describe the processes that student and practice teacher need to follow in order to enable the student to learn. In summary, the model operates as follows.

Students first *retrieve* examples of their practice as raw material for learning. Retrieval may happen in a variety of ways: by using video-tape, written records or discussions. Wherever possible the perspectives of both client and student should be included.

Second, the student *reflects* upon this practice. There are two elements of reflection: examination of the effectiveness of the interaction from the perspectives of both client and social worker; and analysis of values, attitudes and assumptions, expressed through the interaction to make these explicit and understood. Bogo and Vayda recognise that:

> cultural, class, and sex biases and assumptions must be identified so that their influence and power can be understood and controlled. (1987, p. 3)

Third, it is the responsibility of practice teachers to identify sets of theoretical knowledge, and to help students *link* their practice with relevant knowledge. The professional actions taken by students are then analysed and understood within the context of the particular identified theoretical frameworks. Finally, from the understandings gained through exploration of the linkage between action and theory, the nature and quality of *professional responses* can be discussed and evaluated. This leads into further planning and further action with clients.

This four-stage process is then repeated, becoming a continuous process of learning, which throughout the placement links theory and practice in ever more complex and interwoven strands. Bogo and Vayda term this the ITP (Integration of Theory and Practice) loop model.

The role systems model

The role systems model was first identified by Wijnberg and Schwartz. It is built upon three Parsonian concepts of social structures: social roles, the interplay of communications and mechanisms of social control (Wijnberg and Schwartz, 1977). According to the model, relationships between practice teachers and students are defined and circumscribed by social roles, which have the function of creating expectations and imposing identities for participants, that is, as a practice teacher or as a student. Ideally, these role expectations are negotiated and agreed between practice teacher and student, though the practice teacher must be responsible for making explicit those elements of the teacher and student that are essential. Wijnberg and Schwartz assert that the relationship cannot be equal:

> If supervisors give up the 'more knowing stance', it may seem to students that they are not caring, interested, or competent. However, part of the supervisors' competence is to acknowledge when the supervisee has some special capabilities which may, in fact be superior to theirs. (1977, p. 109)

Thus, Wijnberg and Schwartz recognise the existence of an imbalance of power between practice teachers and students, and give the primary responsibility to the practice teacher for ensuring that learning of the most appropriate type occurs. Communication between student and practice teacher is defined in terms of a stimulus to the role system, and negative feedback in either direction is a feature positively regarded as it demonstrates the health of the role system. It is the absence of communication that is undesired! To assist students in such negotiations, Wijnberg and Schwartz provide helpful guidance.

This model incorporates sociological theory and indicates

the importance of negotiation between practice teacher and student.

A structured learning model

A new model of practice learning will be described in subsequent chapters of this book, termed the *structured learning model*. This model of practice learning seeks to provide systematised guidance for practice teachers and students when facing universal issues found on placement, such as:

- how do we decide what the student needs to learn?
- what methods of learning can be used on the placement?
- how might the student's competence to practise be examined?

These questions, and others, require answers. The model builds upon existing good practice and suggests ways that this can be enhanced and strengthened. It is not a *theory* of practice learning but a *model* with a limited scope. However, it may offer a step towards the development of practice learning theory.

The model is grounded in educational principles, and this is not without difficulty. No single unified theory of pedagogy (how to teach) exists that could be easily adapted to fit the needs of practice learning in social work. Rather, there are series of distinct theories and models, each providing partial explanations of particular phenomena or recommending prescriptions that address different elements of learning and teaching. However, it is essential to incorporate insights from these models and theories into learning about social work practice, to improve the process of enabling students to learn, even though there may be substantial disagreement about the relative merits of any particular educational approach or theory, or the weight to be accorded to a given component. Thus, the first step in the development of this model is to recognise the importance of incorporating ideas and models drawn from educational theory into the model of practice learning. The second step is to recognise and validate the current good practice evident in placements, to record this and to strengthen and build upon the principles and ideas being used by practice teachers.

The most important elements of educational theory and models to be incorporated into the structured learning model are as follows.

1. The principles of how people learn

There is a body of research and literature which examines how people can best be taught and enabled to learn. Some of this material suggests that children learn in different ways from adults or that there are various approaches to learning adopted by different people. Opportunities for learning for social work students must accommodate these differences.

The technology of teaching and the experience of the teacher ought not to be confused with the needs of the learner, so that teaching must be understood as related to, but not synonymous with, the process of learning. It is axiomatic that the purpose of practice learning is the development of skills, knowledge and values in practice. This entails that prospective social workers be given opportunities to acquire, develop and use all necessary requirements for day-to-day work in the profession of social work. The structured learning model of practice learning incorporates principles of how people learn skills, knowledge and values drawn from educational theories and models.

2. Planned curriculum

The model incorporates the idea that practice learning can be enhanced through the use of a curriculum to specify what a student needs to learn on placement. Most class-based teaching relies upon an explicit curriculum, defining the content of learning. This curriculum can be consulted by both teacher and student, opening elements of learning to scrutiny. A curriculum imposes a framework upon the body of knowledge to be learned and generates requirements for both the teacher and the learner. Only in recent years has the idea of specifying a detailed and precise curriculum for placements been realised. The curriculum or the content of what students learn on placement can be defined in various ways: through a series of learning objectives; a listing of competencies or a specification of different subject areas to be considered. Important questions then arise about how such a curriculum can be used.

3. Variety of methods of learning

The model suggests that practice teachers and students use a wide variety of methods to learn about social work practice. A rich variety of learning opportunities are presented to students on placement. These have not always been used as effectively as possible to maximise students' learning; for example, there has been a heavy reliance upon discussion by students and practice teachers of a student's work as a method of learning about practice. This is a valid method of enabling learning but there are many others. Using a wide variety of teaching and learning methods can greatly enrich students' experience on placement and improve the quality of their practice.

4. A set of principles to guide the examination of students

Assessment and examination are by nature controversial areas; they are likely to remain so. Measuring whether or not a student is competent to practise social work is a very difficult and demanding task, however it is approached. There is a need to consider a wide range of approaches to examination and how this very difficult task can be made as easy as possible. The model incorporates a series of principles to help students and practice teachers collect and evaluate evidence about the student's practice.

Together, these four elements of practice learning, when combined, generate the structured learning model. In subsequent chapters the implications of this model for practice learning will be fully explored.

4

Understanding Learning

Summary

To begin to develop the structured learning model, practice teachers and students need to incorporate some principles of learning into their approach to practice learning. This is the starting point for the development of the structured learning model. In this chapter basic issues are considered – such as what do we understand by 'learning'. This is a prerequisite to enabling practice learning on placement. Some important educational models are reviewed, to explore the extent to which these can be used on placement. Also some practical checklists and suggestions for practice teachers and students to develop their thinking about learning are given at the end of the chapter.

The nature of learning

Learning about social work practice is at the very heart of a placement: this, after all, is the reason that students have placements. Yet it is often difficult to find the time to ask fundamental questions about the nature of learning on placement, such as 'What is "learning" in a general sense?' or 'How might learning best be enabled on placement?' These may seem to be unnecessary questions, yet unless there is a basic and shared understanding between practice teacher and student about some of the fundamentals of learning there is a considerable danger

53

that the placement will not be successful. The structured learning model suggests that practice teachers and students need to incorporate ideas drawn from educational models and theories, which have generated a very substantial body of knowledge. Only those ideas and principles that are useful should be selected and incorporated into the approach to practice learning adopted on placement. We intend to suggest some principles and explore some educational ideas. However, we would encourage practice teachers and students to seek out other educational principles to add to their lexicon for enabling learning. First, we intend to examine the basic question 'what is learning?'

Asking an apparently simple question, such as 'what is learning?', can produce complex and sometimes confusing responses, because attempts to define the nature of learning are controversial. However, there is one area of agreement in the literature on learning, and that is that for learning to occur there must be a change of some sort in the learner. Yet there is no consensus among learning theorists about the nature of change in learners that is required (Rogers, 1977, p. 58). A modest, easily understood, working definition of learning is succinctly provided by Bernard Lovell. He argues that learning is:

> a relatively permanent change in our potential for performance as the result of our past interaction with the environment. (Lovell, 1980, p. 30)

Here, learning is conceptualised as a product of the individual's relationship with the environment. This interaction produces something new and original to that individual. Hence, learning is a social and an interactive process, not merely an event in the mind. Not all change involves learning; for learning to occur, the change produced must have some durability. Not all change resulting in learning will be for the better (Kidd, 1973, p. 15), since individuals can learn maladaptive, deviant or delinquent behaviour. Siporin restricts the definition of learning to those instances where behaviour is changed in a 'desired direction' (Siporin, 1982, p. 176).

Apart from desired and undesired, two other categories of learning can be distinguished. First, 'incidental learning', where automatic and involuntary responses to new information produce learning. In other words, the learner has little control over the learning that takes place. Second, 'purposeful changes aimed at achieving mastery' in the performance of particular skills. The latter type of learning requires effort and active engagement by the learner (Rogers, 1986, p. 43).

Learning will occur in different areas or aspects of a student's abilities. In an influential paper, Gagné (1972, p. 3) distinguished five 'domains' of learning:

- motor skills
- verbal information
- intellectual skills
- cognitive strategies
- attitudes

This is by no means the only way of conceptualising 'areas' of learning. For example Lewin (1948) differentiates:

- skills
- knowledge
- motivation
- and ideology

while Rogers defines different spheres of learning:

- *skills* – ability to do things
- *knowledge* – memorised information
- *understanding* – relating to memorised information
- *attitudes; wisdom* – 'to learn to apply our newly learned material to what we do and how we live, to carry out our new learning into changed ways of behaving'. (Rogers, 1986, p. 44)

The importance of these distinctions for practice teachers and students lies in the categorisation of different units or parts of learning, whether they are termed 'areas', 'domains' or 'spheres' of learning. Students may learn more easily in some 'areas', 'domains' or 'spheres' than in others. Or they may experience difficulties in learning in some of these categories. Social work is a complex task that requires students to learn a broad range of abilities. Hence, students need to be able to learn in all of the categories in any of the three conceptual schemes, whichever scheme is chosen as being helpful to map different types of learning.

From these different theoretical approaches to understanding learning, it is suggested that learning on placement may be of two kinds:

1. *Type A learning* – a relatively permanent change in the student's potential for performance. This is the product of past, purposeful interactions with the environment and involves effort by the student.
2. *Type B learning* – a relatively permanent change in the student's potential for performance, which is the product of one or several automatic responses to occurrences within the student's environment.

Either of these may be positive or negative in outcome. Positive learning improves the student's ability to perform particular elements of the social work role more effectively, and negative learning detracts from performance of the social work role. Positive type A learning should be the dominant form of student learning if the placement is to be successful. The history of practice learning is littered with many examples of placements dominated by 'incidental learning', that is, where students have been expected to learn by 'soaking it in' – a natural result of 'sitting by Nellie' (solely learning by observation). There is bound to be a balance between the amount of type A learning and type B learning on a placement, but every effort should be made to ensure that the majority of learning is type A.

Over-reliance upon type B learning runs two great risks. First, students' learning may not be predominantly positive – it will have *random*, not planned, outcomes. Second, the time available to a student on placement is limited, therefore opportunities for learning need to be maximised so that the pace of learning is as fast as possible, commensurate with the student's ability to learn. This will not occur where learning is *ad hoc*.

Theories of learning

There are a great many theories about learning; these vary in scope and theoretical context from analyses of childhood intellectual development (Piaget, 1953, for example) to sociological critiques of power relationships in education (Illich, 1971, for example). Our concern is not to review the full literature on learning theories, but to examine theories which have influenced practice learning, or those that might contribute to our understanding of learning about social work practice.

Process models of learning

A *process model* of learning identifies different stages or processes that a student is likely to experience during a placement or on a social work course. Often these models include the likely emotional responses that students might have as they progress through a placement. There have been many examples of process models of learning in social work education, as Siporin, in mildly critical vein, notes:

> The characteristic fondness of social workers for process conceptions of teaching has led to a long line of published efforts that describe the teaching–learning enterprise, including field instruction [practice teaching] in process terms. (1982, p. 181)

One of the first influential process models of learning in social work was propounded by Bertha Reynolds in 1942. She described four different stages of consciousness encountered by students whilst learning a task. These are:

- 'acute consciousness of self' (feel unable to complete tasks and may experience flight or fight responses)
- 'sink or swim adaptation' (possession of a hazy notion of what is required)
- 'a sense of understanding intellectually what is required without the power to control his or her activity within it' (the ability to complete the action repeatedly is very uneven or patchy)
- 'relative mastery' (when a task can be completed with competence and the individual's perception of their ability is correct)

To learn how to complete a task successfully a student needs to engage with these different stages. Finally, when the student has achieved competence in the skill in question, a further development is possible, and that is the ability to teach the skill to others. This ability can only be achieved when preoccupation with the content of the subject is overcome, allowing the teacher to concentrate on the needs of those wishing to learn (Reynolds, 1942, pp. 75–85).

The danger implicit in this and other similar process models is that they become set in concrete. Both student and practice teacher may expect a student to progress dutifully and systematically through each of the stages in prescribed order. Failure to do so may be interpreted as a failure of students to learn. In outlining these stages of learning, Reynolds did not expect students to pass through them in a 'well-marked order', yet she did expect that:

> progress from one stage to another however, should be discernible in general. (1942, p. 74)

Students approach learning in a variety of different ways, according to previous educational experience, personality, ethnicity, gender, class, and so on. It is not, therefore, to be expected that they will all learn in the same way. Where a model of learning generates, or reinforces, the belief that there is only one approach to learning, linked to a series of stages or processes, its value is counterproductive. Students who do not progress in the predicted pattern may be seen as failing. As Siporin again comments:

> the idealised quality of many of these sequential stage presentations has made them useful in the inevitable games student and instructors [practice teachers] play. At prescribed times, some students offer to the field instructor the desired and expected responses of successive anxiety, elation, depression, self-derogation, self-confidence and so on. (1982, p. 181)

However, this type of model may be useful as a framework that allows both student and practice teacher to classify the student's behaviour and performance, without inferring that progress must take a predetermined pattern. Another group of models begin by considering differences in the ways that students learn and seek to provide methods to help students use these differences positively.

Learning styles and strategies

In the past twenty years there has been an increased interest in the idea of learning itself and a variety of books have been published, amongst them many popular 'self-help' books to enable readers to improve their learning skills (Buzan, 1974; Rowntree, 1976). Underlying these and other books is a considerable body of empirical research into learning. Reviewing this area of literature, Newble and Entwistle have distinguished two broad streams of thinking. In North American research, they find an emphasis on how personality traits influence learning, particularly the idea that individuals have *learning styles* – relatively stable attributes of the individual that determine the way in which he or she learns – whilst European and Australian literature explores ways in which different students approach learning tasks in everyday situations – individuals adopt different *learning strategies* (Newble and Entwistle, 1986). Some of this research challenges beliefs that ability to learn is an innate faculty. If correct, then there is the possibility that skills involved in efficient and effective learning can be taught and themselves learned. This research has considerable implications for practice teachers and students on placement. If it is possible to develop skills in learning, then, given that the placement is a relatively unique learning experience, students may need help in developing the necessary skills to maximise their practice learning.

Learning styles

The research into learning styles seeks to classify people into certain types, according to the way in which they prefer to learn. This learning style specifies the types of activity that a person finds most effective as a vehicle for learning. A learning style is intended to record how people have learned in the past and to predict how they will respond to new situations. Also the learning style may be regarded as a relatively stable attribute of personality and therefore not amenable to much change. The identification of an individual's learning style typically depends on responses given to a set number of questions, or preferences for words or images. For example Kolb, one of the founders of this approach, developed the Learning Styles Inventory (LSI), which requires individuals to respond to 36 individual words. Depending upon the responses given, individuals are designated as having one of four distinct learning styles. These are defined as Converger, Diverger, Assimilator and Accomodator (Kolb, 1976). The precise characteristics of each category need not concern us greatly as according to one reviewer, in 1983, there were no less than 21 different testing schedules, each supposedly measuring learning style (Curry, 1983). No doubt since that review was conducted many more have been devised.

One version of the learning styles method has been used by a number of practice teachers in the UK – this is the Learning Styles Questionnaire (LSQ) devised by Honey and Mumford (1986). The LSQ which builds upon the work of Kolb, was originally intended for use with managers to identify individual managers' learning styles, but can be used with other groups. The LSQ is a self-completion questionnaire that contains some 80 statements, each marked by respondents according to whether they agree or disagree. Depending upon which statements the respondent agrees/disagrees with, a score is given and dominant features of a particular individual's learning style can be identified by comparison with norms of a wider sample group. Four different learning styles have been identified by Honey and Mumford: Activist, Reflector, Theorist and Pragmatist. They are characterised as follows:

- *Activists* are enthusiastic for new experiences, and tend to be dominated by their immediate focus of attention. They welcome new challenges but become bored by implementation and consolidation. They may rush hastily into activities and tend to centre everything upon themselves, including group discussion

- *Reflectors* observe and evaluate experiences from several different perspectives, collecting much data and considering many alternatives before deciding upon a course of action. They tend to be thoughtful and cautious and adopt a low profile in meetings and group discussions, often getting the drift of a discussion before making their own points. They may seem to be distant, but tolerant

- *Theorists* mould their observations into complex and logically sound theories. They think problems through in a systematic, step-by-step manner. Often they are perfectionists who cannot rest until things conform to their view. They like to analyse and synthesise and have a preference for basic assumptions, principles, theories, models and systems thinking. The approach they adopt may be detached and analytical, and they tend to prefer certainty to subjective judgement. The ability to think laterally may be poorly developed

- *Pragmatists* enjoy experimentation and the practical application of ideas and theories, testing their validity in the day-to-day world. They like to act quickly and with confidence, and dislike open-ended discussion, preferring active problem-solving. Opportunities are seen as a challenge, and they tend to look for better ways of doing things

According to Honey and Mumford, individuals may have one style that predominates over others in their learning. They also suggest that possession of a particular learning style predisposes the individual to learn best from a given range of activities. For example, activists learn best from activities such as role-play, team-work tasks and so on. Similarly they learn badly from more passive methods such as reading, watching demonstrations or lectures. No learning style is better or necessarily more desirable than any other and each has strengths and weaknesses. If an individual has a strong preference for a particular style of learning, then that person will learn most effectively when the programme of learning resonates with their preferred learning style. Learning will be ineffective and inefficient where the converse is the case.

What use can be made of this model of learning by practice teachers and students? It can be used as part of a placement to help students identify their own preferred style of learning. Depending upon the results, learning experiences on placement can be arranged, as far as possible, to coincide with the student's preferred learning style.

However, the LSQ should be used with some caution. The work of Honey and Mumford may be criticised on two grounds. First, is the model that they use applicable to and valid for social work students? In their own evaluation, Honey and Mumford were cautious about the status of their work, suggesting that their main concern:

> has not been to produce something that is academically respectable, but to produce something which will give detailed practical guidance to those who are trying to develop their abilities and to those who are trying to help them. (1986, p. 5)

The empirical studies upon which their findings are based consisted of managers, only a tiny proportion of whom were women and with no indication of how many were black or from other minority groups. Care is therefore needed when applying their results to a very diverse group such as social work students. At the very least there are substantial questions about the extent to which their work can be directly applicable to social work students on placement without further empirical study.

The second criticism applies to the learning styles methodology in general; this model can be taken to suggest that an individual's learning style is something relatively firm and fixed. If this is the case, then practice teachers may be inclined to try to present a student only with learning opportunities that closely match the student's learning style. If pursued rigorously this might not encourage the student to develop new approaches to learning. It is unclear how far, within the terms of this model, students can change their learning style. This is the most substantial criticism of the group of learning styles models.

Learning strategies

We can understand the term *learning strategy* to refer to the approach adopted by a student when given a particular piece of material to learn. Learning strategies are distinct from learning styles in that they do not form part of the personality, but are selected by the individual when confronted by a learning task. Individuals may possess an extensive or limited range of strategies, and may be inclined to use some strategies more frequently than others.

We might ask whether an individual student has a tendency to adopt the same learning strategy when confronted by different learning tasks? If this is the case, then on some occasions the student will be successful in learning, on other occasions the student's success is likely to be limited. Are some learning strategies more useful in learning some tasks than others? Pask (1976) addressed these questions, and suggested that students do have a preferred learning strategy – an approach to learning that each individual tends to adopt in the majority of learning situations. He argued that some students are disposed to act as 'holists', and these he termed 'comprehension learners'. They demonstrate a tendency to build descriptions of what may be known. Others are disposed to 'serialist' approaches: these are 'operation learners' who seek to grasp procedural detail (Entwistle, 1978). There are also students who are able to move between these different learning strategies with relative ease, having 'versatile' approaches to learning.

What are the implications of Pask's work for social work students' practice learning and can these ideas help practice teachers and students on placement? To identify an individual's learning strategies, Pask used an imaginative if complex test; students were asked to work out taxonomies for imaginary Martian animals called 'Clobbits'. As part of his research into practice learning, Gardiner used the 'Clobbits' test with fifteen pairs of practice teachers and students to identify differences in learning strategies between practice teachers and students. This appears to be the only reported usage of the 'Clobbits' test in relation to practice learning (Gardiner, 1989, p. 71). According to Gardiner, there is wide agreement that where teaching methods correspond with a student's preferred learning strategy, the student's learning achievements will be enhanced. Conversely, where there is mismatch, students are likely to perform less well.

There are clear implications here for both student and practice teacher. First, both need to be aware of the existence and importance of preferred learning strategies. All too frequently, it is assumed that students automatically possess such meta-skills as the ability to learn effectively, and that students have the innate capacity to learn in a variety of ways. Second, if there is persistent mismatch between the teaching style and the preferred learning strategy, the student is, in effect, being taught to fail. Third, the practice teacher can encourage the student to develop a range of learning strategies. A student's preferred learning strategy is not some fixed characteristic but may be seen as a skill to be developed. Fourth, Entwistle (1978) suggests that we must be tentative in applying Pask's work. It has been most successfully used in various scientific disciplines where there are widely agreed conceptual frameworks. This is not necessarily the case in social work, where there is considerable diversity of opinion about the nature, context and content of practice (Payne, 1991), and there is no dominant paradigm for social work as there is for many other social sciences (Kuhn, 1970).

A student may choose to become an 'all-round learner' by developing competence in a broad range of different learning strategies, and this is the most desirable approach to learning on placement. To develop this versatility it may be necessary for practice teachers and students to devise a range of exercises designed to strengthen particular learning strategies. These exercises resemble the intellectual equivalent of a good workout in the gym!

Malcolm Knowles and adult learning

A significant and influential contribution to thinking about learning in social work has been made by Malcolm Knowles. His model of andragogy, the art and science of helping adults to learn, has been enthusiastically embraced – sometimes uncritically – in the field of practice learning.

Knowles's theories are based upon two fundamental principles: first, that much of what is known about the way learning occurs has been derived from studies of children and animals (Knowles, 1970); second, that methods of promoting learning in the education system (United States) are regressive, becoming worse from nursery school through to college. He makes this argument because in his opinion *all* education is dominated by pedagogy, the art and science of teaching children, and so becomes less suitable as children become adults as they progress through the educational system (Knowles, 1972). Pedagogy, according to Knowles, is a model of teaching where the purpose of education is the 'transmission of culture' or the archaic 'transmission of knowledge' (1970, p. 37). In such a model, the role of the teacher is to know more than the learner and to teach a prescribed body of knowledge.

Challenging the applicability of these principles of education for adults, and drawing on the work of adult education theorists, particularly in Germany, the former Yugoslavia and the United States, Knowles proposes a new technology for educating adults, called andragogy, the art and science of helping adults to learn (1970, p. 38). Knowles's model for adult learning introduces a range of principles about teaching, which serve as guidelines for good practice in enabling adults to learn. Importantly, he wrote directly about the application of these principles to social work education (1972). Some of the more important principles, derived from his work, can be applied to learning on placement. These principles for good practice are as follows:

- *Learning climate*   The physical milieu of the learning environment must be congenial, relaxing and comfortable to reduce anxiety and promote and heighten receptivity to learning. Even more important is the creation of a psychological environment where the learner feels:

    accepted, respected and supported; in which there exists a spirit of mutuality between teachers and students as joint inquirers; in which there is freedom of expression without fear of punishment or ridicule. (Knowles, 1970, p. 41)

- *Diagnosis of needs*   Students must self-diagnose their learning needs; motivation for learning will only be present where students are committed to the relevance of the content of learning and to its final outcome
- *The planning process*   Students must be involved in the planning of their own learning to translate diagnosed learning needs into specific educational objectives
- *Conducting learning experiences*   The traditional model of a teacher with sole responsibility for the content of the learning transactions and the learner as passive recipient of what the teacher chooses to offer is rejected. Instead the teacher becomes an enabler, a facilitator who assists another to learn:

    In fact the teacher's role is redefined as that of a procedural technician, resource person, and co-inquirer; he is more a catalyst than an instructor, more a guide than a wizard. (Knowles, 1970, p. 43)

- *Emphasis on experiential techniques* Adults have much to contribute to the learning of others, and are a rich resource for learning; adults have a substantial foundation of past experience, which can be related to present experience and is a source of meaning and context for learning. Conversely, adults will have a tendency to adopt fixed habits and modes of thinking and so may not be receptive to new ideas. Use can be made of the experience of adults to enrich the learning environment, and their experience can contribute much to the learning techniques adopted. Greater use of a variety of techniques including group discussion, simulation exercises, role-play, practice exercises, projects, active demonstration and so on is possible
- *Emphasis on practical application* Illustrations from experiences relevant to the learner can be incorporated into conceptualisations presented as part of the learning process. Even better if these can be drawn directly from the learner's experience. In addition, the learner can plan how to rehearse and apply the content of learning in practice. This helps to reinforce learning
- *The timing of learning* The key concept for organising the timing is not the logic of an abstract syllabus, but the actual concerns of the students at a particular point in approaching a subject or skill area. There is a parallel with the developmental stages of the young child, who can only learn to walk when the sensory motor system is ready to acquire this particular skill. So, in the case of an adult, specific learning will only occur when the subject-matter is directly relevant to the concerns of the learner
- *Design of learning experiences* Knowles suggests that the most usual starting point for a particular learning sequence is not to begin with statements about the content of the programme, but by asking what the learners wish to get out of the programme. He acknowledges that the issues the learners are aware of at the start is

the beginning, not the end, of the learning experience. This does not constrain the content of learning

In these statements, derived from Knowles's work, there
are substantial practice guidelines which students and practice teachers can use on placements. A major importance
of Knowles's work lies in his redefinition of the roles of
teacher and learner. Locating responsibility to learn with
the student fits well with traditional social work ideologies,
which place importance on autonomy and self-direction.
Nevertheless, the primary responsibility for the creation
and maintenance of a favourable learning climate must
rest initially with the practice teacher.

Despite the importance of Knowles's work, it may be
criticised on at least two counts. First, much has not been
empirically tested. On the other hand, if his ideas provide a useful analysis and valuable prescriptions, then they
ought not to be rejected, at least until something else
which is more useful, or has been more rigorously tested,
is available. Second, his work has been criticised for not
taking account of the range of prior experiences of a wide
enough group of learners and because his approach is
both gender-specific, primarily designed for male learners,
and also class-specific for middle-class learners (Humphries,
1988).

Learning and the structured learning model

A first step in the construction of the structured learning
model is an acknowledgement that models and theories
of how people learn ought to play an important part in
informing what happens to students on placement, such
that students' and practice teachers' approaches to practice learning are informed by these models and theories.

So far in this chapter, we have selected a few examples
of important models which have implications for practice
learning. Of course, there are many others. We hope that
students and practice teachers will identify their own approaches and use a wide variety of models drawn from

educational theory. The structured learning model only suggests that these should be the starting point for the construction of practice learning. It does not prescribe those models that should or should not be used.

To begin to develop the model we propose three principles about learning.

Principle one

The structured learning model is grounded in a belief in the importance of educational principles and philosophies. These encompass a wide range of different theories and models. Individual practice teachers and students need to evaluate their own orientation to these different principles and to decide how to incorporate them into their approach to learning.

Principle two

Individuals use different learning strategies when approaching any learning task (Pask, 1976). If students' learning is be maximised then all students need to develop a wide range of learning strategies that will allow them to learn from the breadth of learning opportunities available as part of the placement. A task for the practice teacher is to help students to develop competence in a range of learning strategies. It is very easy to assume that students arrive on placement with skills in learning. To help students develop their learning skills, practice teachers need, initially, to help students identify the learning skills that they possess and then to work jointly with the student to devise ways of developing new learning strategies or improving old ones.

Principle three

In helping students to develop their learning strategies to maximise learning on placement full account must be taken of their past experiences of learning. These need to be understood in the context of students' personal biographies and their experience of socially structured difference.

These core principles help to guide the student and practice teacher into using the structured learning model. To help practice teachers and students implement these principles on placement we wish to offer some practical exercises.

Learning practical skills

Based upon the experience of a series of workshops about what helps people to learn about social work, and drawing upon the three principles of practice learning, we have included some practical suggestions:

- a series of skills for practice teachers to help promote students' learning
- some frequently mentioned learning needs for students that can be incorporated as part of the placement
- a suggestion for students to begin to consider their own approach to learning

These are offered as examples of how to promote and maximise learning and can be used in various ways by practice teachers and students. They are not definitive statements about good practice.

Checklist for teacher skills to promote learning

1. Do you offer *encouragement* to learners to overcome hesitancy and to achieve their full potential?
2. Can you provide *honest feedback* to the learner about the progress being made, whilst incorporating key principles of good feedback? These might be taken to include:
   (a) commenting upon behaviour, not attributes of the person;

(b) referring to specific aspects of behaviour that are amenable to change;

(c) remembering that the purpose of feedback is to provide assistance to the recipient not emotional relief for the donor;

(d) concentrating upon positive ways of improvement rather than negative criticism;

(e) avoiding giving specific prescriptive advice; exploring a range of possible options allowing the recipient to decide on a response.

3. Are you willing for students to observe you practising social work to *provide a model* of competent practice, and do you have the skills to help students prepare to observe practice?

4. Do you have the skills to *explain* complex aspects of policy or practice, bringing these to life with metaphor and imagery?

5. Do you routinely check that your assumptions about meaning, use of language and principles are made *explicit* in dialogue with learners, and what skills do you use to do this?

Add your own modifications to these skills!

Checklist of frequently mentioned learners' needs

1. Learners need *recognition of their existing strengths*, so that it is not assumed that they are 'starting from scratch' in everything they do. Learners can also be teachers in some parts of the work.

2. Learners need to be given *guided practice*; after checking their understanding about expectations, learners can be given an opportunity to practise the skill in question in a controlled environment under the close supervision of a teacher. Otherwise, the learner may be given too much responsibility when inadequately prepared. Guided practice

also implies the possibility of a dialogue between the student and the teacher during the process of practising the skill.

3. The student ought not be placed in situations *beyond their level of competence.*

4. Students need to be given the opportunity to *learn complex tasks in small steps,* to make learning complex tasks more simple. Tasks may be broken into smaller units, which may be learned and practised over a period of time. It is important to note that the student need not learn to do these tasks in the sequential order in which they are usually performed. It may be difficult to begin a particular sequence of skilled activity and there is no reason why the practice teacher cannot complete the initial steps on behalf of the student if these are judged to be the most difficult. The component parts of a task may be learned in any order, provided that the student can perform them in the correct order at the point of examination.

5. Learners need demonstrations of competent practice to replicate. Without *examples of observed practice* to analyse and imitate or improve upon, the novice social worker will have to depend solely on intuitive modes of skill performance. Developing competent practice will take much longer than necessary and, ultimately, the student's overall professional development will be hampered through the lack of alternative approaches to practice.

6. Students, however competent, need to feel like acrobats over a *safety net,* where mistakes can be made without disastrous consequences.

7. Where ways of learning are ineffective with particular students it is necessary to *experiment with different approaches,* change tactics and be creative.

8. Many experiences of learning occur as children; practice teachers need to avoid, if possible, reawakening these feelings in students. It is very easy for the teacher to infantalise the learner with disastrous consequences.

9. Recognise that the learner may feel *self-conscious in the process of learning.*

Add your learning needs to this list!

At the start of a placement it is common to ask the students to identify their learning needs. Often, this is limited to the content of what the students want to learn rather than the students' views of the process of learning itself. It is possible to ask the students to identify their approach to learning at this stage. For instance, students can be asked to complete one of the psychological questionnaires described earlier, as a vehicle to help them discover their learning style or learning strategies. Another method of enabling students to explore individual approaches to learning is to complete a brief checklist, either in discussion in a practice tutorial, in a group learning setting, or as a written exercise.

Thinking about learning

Think of a positive example from your past learning where you learned a practical skill or sport (e.g., driving, knitting, swimming, football, basketball, tennis).
Recall how you learned the skills and then list the factors that made this a positive learning experience.
1. How would you like to see these factors included in learning about social work practice on placement?
2. How do you approach learning tasks (think about what you like to do first and what comes next)?
3. What do you find easy to learn, and why?
4. What do you find difficult to learn and why?
5. Do you approach all learning tasks in the same way with the same skills?
6. How would you like to develop your learning skills on placement?

To be effective as learners, students require an understanding of their own abilities to learn. This is a key aspect for practice teacher and student to explore jointly. In practice settings, a great many opportunities for learning exist. Students need to develop abilities in a wide range of learning methods and the acquisition of such a range may be one function of the practice learning opportunities on placement.

Towards a model of practice learning

Writing in 1966 Jerome Bruner commented:

> One is struck by the absence of a theory of instruction as a guide to pedagogy – a prescriptive theory of how to proceed in order to achieve various results, a theory that is neutral with respect to ends but exhaustive with respect to means. It is interesting that there is a lack of integrating theory in pedagogy, that in its place there is principally a body of maxims. (p. 31)

If these words still convey with force our level of understanding about general education, they are particularly apposite in the context of practice learning. It is hardly surprising that we do not have a coherent theory of teaching and learning social work practice. This chapter has examined some aspects of learning, to form a foundation for the other elements of the structured learning model. Without some understanding of the nature of learning, we have no firm footing on which to construct models of practice learning.

A grand theory of learning remains elusive, so we must resort to the fragments of knowledge grounded in theory and practice that are available to us. What remains essential is that practice teachers and students discuss their differing understandings and experiences of learning and use these to promote a framework for learning on placement.

5

Using a Curriculum for Practice Learning

Summary

A core question for all practice teachers and students concerns the nature and type of learning on a placement. This chapter considers the ways in which practice learning can be structured through a practice curriculum. The curriculum's position as a key element in the structured learning model is discussed for practice teachers and students, and various approaches to the design of curricula are reviewed. Principles are presented to aid in devising, developing or modifying curricula for particular contexts.

Towards a practice curriculum

All practice teachers and students face a dilemma in organising the learning that will occur during a placement. Without an organising framework, learning in any field of endeavour is reduced to the accumulation of a stew of ideas, skills, knowledge, aptitudes, values, dispositions and so on. Hence, the practice teacher and student must decide which elements of social work practice will be included as topics for learning and which will be excluded. For some practice teachers and students this will be delineated by the social work course, which prescribes in some way the learning that should occur on

75

placement. For example, if the course uses a competency-based model, the student will have a list of competencies to be achieved during the placement. In some instances, practice teacher and students will negotiate these competencies themselves.

Another approach to specifying what will be learned on placement employs a practice curriculum. The concept of curriculum is familiar enough when applied in the context of class teaching (it specifies what is to be learned in a course) but much less so in regard to practice. Until relatively recently, the idea of 'curriculum' would have seemed strange in conjunction with the notion of practice learning. As the notion of curriculum is explored, it will become evident that it refers to rather more than the content of learning. However, for the moment we will let the notion of a practice curriculum be understood to mean the *content* of what a student learns on placement, to provide a helpful tool for practice teachers and students. The structured learning model uses a practice curriculum to organise the learning on placement, and we advocate its use because it has many advantages for both students and practice teachers.

Class-based teaching in social work education has long used the idea of curriculum to make learning manageable. 'Units' of content provide an underlying structure that helps in the selection of teaching methods: for example, subject areas such as Law, Social Policy, Psychology and Social Work Practice are divided into smaller units, each consisting of a topic of learning. So, Law might include topics of learning such as Emergency Protection Orders or Parental Responsibility. These topics can be harmonised with other topics in other subject areas to achieve a balance across all components of learning. Similar organisational principles are applied to create a practice curriculum. However, a full appreciation of the value of a practice learning curriculum has been made difficult until recently by several factors.

1. A belief in universalism

Until recently, practice teachers have tacitly accepted that they can achieve the impossible: that is, on a placement, a practice teacher could teach a student everything there is to be known about social work practice in a particular setting. On subsequent placements, students would be taught similar material by another practice teacher, the sole difference being that learning would occur within the context of a new setting. As a result, placements have been repetitive. Practice teachers have not easily been able to limit the range of material taught on placement, and a sense of progress in learning for a student, over two or three placements, might not derive so much from developing new and diverse skills, acquiring new knowledge and increased confidence in professional values, or achieving an ability to undertake work of increasing complexity, as from working with different client groups in diverse settings (see Doel, 1988).

This inability to limit the amount that a practice teacher is expected to enable students to learn has been detrimental to the development of a more organised approach to a practice curriculum.

2. The untidiness of social work practice

In the actual world of practice, social work is sometimes seen as too 'messy' and 'untidy' to provide opportunities to structure learning adequately. For example, a practice teacher cannot ensure that clients will deliver the kind of learning opportunities that a student might need at the required time. If a curriculum requires a student to complete a court report in week eight of the placement, how can the practice teacher be sure that one will materialise? The difficulty of relating learning to available experiences rests upon another assumption, that learning is only possible by direct work with clients. We will examine this assumption more closely later.

Leaving aside the problem about how to provide a certain type of learning experience at a particular time, it is clear that the practice teacher is less likely to realise that a particular learning experience is missing in the absence of a curriculum. The belief that learning about social work practice cannot be structured through a practice curriculum needs to be challenged.

3. Over-use of traditional methods of learning

A predominant approach to teaching students on placement has been the traditional method of learning by discussion of practice with practice teachers. Such an approach to teaching derives from the notion of 'practice as too messy a business to structure for learning'. Whilst this belief prevails, there is no real opportunity to develop and devise a practice curriculum, because the activity of learning about social work practice is not located within a conceptual framework of teaching and learning.

4. Nature of the relationship between class- and practice-based learning

Another factor preventing the development of a curriculum-based approach has been an uncertainty about the purpose of placements and their relationship to the parts of the courses taught in class. Traditionally, the placement has been regarded as an opportunity for students to apply in practice what has been learned in the classroom (Parsloe, 1983). If this view, or something similar, is accepted there is very little purpose in structuring the practice learning opportunities through a curriculum, because the *required* curriculum is delivered in the class-based component to the course.

This viewpoint, which asserts that class teaching is paramount and practice secondary, has been reinforced by other factors that give precedence to the class components of social work courses. The nature of the relationship between college tutors and practice teachers is such that the former tend to have greater access to information about the course, more control over the programme of learning, and their employment is related to the programme or course. In contrast, practice teachers have been, all too often, on the periphery of the programme and unable to assert the interests of practice learning. This position is changing and may mean practice teachers are more able to influence the shape of social work courses.

These assumptions are being challenged; for example, by a recent collection of papers which asserts that the curriculum for social work education should be led by practice (Phillipson, Richards and Sawdon, 1988). A practice curriculum has many advantages; some of the most important are given below.

Advantages of a practice curriculum

- The requirements of social work practice can shape the content of what is learned by students through a practice curriculum
- Students are empowered through the existence of an explicit written practice curriculum; they can have an understanding of required learning at the start of the placement
- Practice teachers are empowered through the development of the curriculum as 'a common currency', so there is an opportunity and a reason to become connected with each other
- It is possible to organise practice learning so that simple or core skills, basic knowledge or fundamental values are learned before the more complex elements of practice are attempted
- It is possible with a practice curriculum to know when learning has been achieved in given areas, and then to move on to other components of the curriculum or to find ways to compensate for deficiencies in the learning environment – if, for example, live practice with clients is not generating appropriate learning experiences, other methods of learning can be used
- The curriculum allows for a range of different learning

> opportunities and learning methods to be used: these can be well-organised and planned before the start of the placement
> - The examination of practice competence can be structured and harmonised to fit with the pace of learning

If these are the advantages of a practice curriculum, we may then ask 'what does a practice curriculum look like?'

Defining practice curricula: some examples

The word curriculum literally means 'a course to be run' and derives from the course around which Roman chariots raced. At first thought, a curriculum may simply appear to be a given list of items of knowledge that a student is required to learn on placement. However, this view belies the complexity that underlies the notion of curriculum, for as Bruner suggests:

> A curriculum should involve the mastery of skills that in turn lead to the mastery of still more powerful ones, the establishment of self reward sequences. (1966, p. 35)

Grundy argues that curriculum is not an abstract concept, with independent existence, external to the human experience; it is a cultural construction which provides a framework for 'organising a set of human educational practices' (1987, p. 5). Taking just these two views, it is clear that the notion of curriculum is complex.

For the purposes of the practice teacher and student thinking about a practice curriculum, something practical and helpful is needed. Let us consider some real examples of practice curricula to begin to define the nature of a curriculum for practice learning. In the field of practice learning some examples of curricula have been published and are widely available. Three examples of these curricula have been selected and are described, illustrating different approaches to the notion of practice curriculum.

The 'three spheres' model

Margaret Richards has outlined a practice curriculum which organises and classifies practice learning into three distinct 'spheres' – primary, secondary and tertiary (1987, 1988). A 'sphere' is a domain of learning that contains groups of skills and defined areas of knowledge. These spheres are not ordered in a hierarchy, nor is any one more or less fundamental than the others, but they provide a broad framework for the organisation of learning (Doel, 1988). It does not matter which of the spheres is addressed first by students but, by the end of the course, a student is expected to have achieved a 'beginning' level of competence in the skills and knowledge contained in each of these spheres:

- The *primary sphere* encompasses work with social groups who may not be able to meet their basic needs for living. The knowledge and skills required in this sphere are principally various forms of group work, and these skills prepare students to enable individuals to develop their own abilities in fulfilling their needs
- The *secondary sphere* is characterised as the most readily recognisable as social work for which people are currently trained (Richards, 1987, p. 7). The focus for learning is on the skills needed to work with individuals who have become alienated from essential social roles; the causes of such dislocation are disparate and may include deviancy, loss, illness and so on. When working in this sphere, the social worker will be engaged in the assessment of risk and may become involved in issues of social control
- In the *tertiary sphere*, major emphasis is given to situations where individuals require '24 hours' coverage', irrespective of whether this requirement for care arises from individuals living in an institution, in substitute family care, or in their own home in the community.

A principle task for social workers in this area of practice is to minimise damage to the individual's self-es-
teem and to maintain their sense of identity

Richards recognises that her conceptualisation of the curriculum may appear to be a repackaging of the historic
division between group work, casework and residential work.
She denies this view and asserts that social workers cannot practise effectively without a thorough understanding
of the distinct skills, knowledge and values contained in
each sphere. In a later paper, Richards suggests the need
for a foundation unit to give an overview of required learning and to begin to enable students to understand issues
of power, discrimination and oppression. These themes
run through each of the subsequent spheres (Richards,
1988, p. 69).

The spheres approach to curriculum specifies the areas
of knowledge and skill that a student must acquire, but it
does not convey a 'technology' of how students might
progress through these required components of learning.

The 'matrix' model

In their approach to a practice curriculum, Butler and
Elliot (1985) seek to create a framework which is sufficiently
complex and flexible to accommodate the wide variety of
social work practice. To achieve this they organise the
curriculum by constructing a paradigm model (Doel, 1988).
The paradigm consists of a framework to organise all the
required skills and knowledge for social work practice.
Their curriculum consists of a matrix with three dimensions: skill areas, life situations, and practice contexts.
Together, these dimensions locate all of the essential
knowledge, skills and values needed for social work practice. They identify different segments or 'cells' of learning. In the first dimension, there are five *skill areas*:

- thinking
- feeling
- communication

- processing work through time
- learning skills

These skill areas are required in all social work activities and need to be applied in twelve basic *life situations*:

- beginnings
- dependency
- ambivalence
- conflict
- group contact
- unhappiness in relationships
- deficiencies
- crisis
- achievement
- illness
- deterioration
- endings and loss

These elements of learning represent a complete range of life situations that social workers encounter in their practice. All of these situations occur in one of four different *contexts of practice*:

- the place of self
- one or two people
- in and between groups
- within and between agencies and institutions

Butler and Elliot represent this curriculum as a three-dimensional matrix, with some 240 distinct cells, each as a distinct curriculum element. In theory, it is possible to identify these discrete cells within the matrix, and to make explicit the learning required to achieve competence in that given area of practice.

Example

A student placed in a residential unit for children, about to begin a new piece of group work, would consult the cell delineated by the dimensions 'beginnings', 'in and between groups' and 'communication'. This would define the skills and knowledge the student would need to acquire for this piece of practice. (It is highly likely that the student would also need to consult the other four skill areas to have a full grasp of what might be entailed by starting a group.)

According to Butler and Elliot, the importance of the practice curriculum rests upon two factors: the basic function of learning in social work education is to enable practitioners to acquire knowledge and experience; and the ability to identify similarities between situations in terms of the knowledge appropriate to them. The paradigm approach provides a clear plan for organising the content of the curriculum, but its use in everyday practice is complex because of the very large number of parts to the curriculum.

The 'building block' model

Doel has described a model of practice curriculum, which we have termed here the 'building block' model (1987a, 1988). This model describes the content of a curriculum for practice over three periods of practice learning, but the same principles can be applied to any number of placements. The particular example organises the content of the learning into six units, two for each placement. Each unit represents the clustering of broad themes in the curriculum.

First placement

Unit A: Working in the agency – skills of personal organisation

This incorporates elements that have been described as the 'nature of a professional relationship', 'values in social work' and 'organisational skills'. The emphasis here is upon the student's self and the way in which this influences the work done and how students present themselves to others. Other skills are included such as the beginning skills of working in an agency, where there are often conflicting and confusing demands made upon students' time.

Unit B: Initial skills – engaging others

This unit addresses interactional skills in working with other people – the 'bricks and mortar' of social work interventions. The ability to communicate skilfully with people is fundamental to social work and without this foundation, a student's future work is shaky or even impossible.

Second placement

Unit C: Social work methods – skills in helping others over time

A social work method is a high-order skill, and consists of activities which have a prescribed, coherent sequence and stand on a researched and tested theoretical base. Students need to develop a working knowledge of at least one social work method, not as an exclusive way of working, but as the beginning of the acquisition of competence in a variety of different methods of practice.

Unit D: Work with different users – skills of generic practice

Students must demonstrate an ability to work with clients and users with different attributes – people of different 'race', age, gender and so on, and with a variety of different problems. No categorisation of these groups is entirely satisfactory, but account must be taken of the ability to transfer life situations (for example, the notion of crisis) from one group to another.

Third placement

Unit E: Working in the agency – skills of influencing others

In unit A, the student practised the skills of personal organisation necessary to work successfully in an agency. In this unit the focus is on a broader and deeper knowledge of the organisation and the skills necessary to work effectively as a team member in a broader agency.

Unit F: Working in and with groups – skills of working with many others

Much of the student's learning has so far been limited to work with individuals or families. In this unit the focus for learning moves to larger contexts – not just groups 'created' by social workers, but teams, communities and neighbourhood groups, group care and organisational groups such as special interest groups and agency working parties.

Each of the units is split into smaller parts or modules, approximately four to six in each unit. This clusters the learning into manageable pieces. The significance of this type of curriculum rests not in the precise content, but in the provision of an underlying structure and principles for organising practice learning. Some of the key principles incorporated in this type of curriculum are as follows.

Codification of good practice

The 'building block' curriculum does not begin with a 'grand design' and then attempt to fit practice learning into a given framework. Instead, it is grounded on the imperatives of good practice and ways in which these can be brought together. This curriculum is not, therefore, an edifice imposed upon practice, but an attempt to codify the kinds of activities that students might well have performed as part of a placement. It is organically constructed from practice by drawing and grouping together similar kinds of knowledge and skills. These pieces of learning, called modules, can be assembled into larger units, so this type of practice curriculum builds incrementally, opening up the possibility of innovation and improving the curriculum. Items can be discarded or modified at will, according to changes in practice. The building block curriculum is not fixed and unchanging.

Integration with classroom learning

Whichever route to developing a practice curriculum is taken, the resulting definition of the content of learning on placement opens up the possibility of integrating the student's experience of learning across class and practice settings. In the absence of a curriculum for practice, the content of learning on placement may be sporadic, random and piecemeal, without these disadvantages becoming apparent to either the teacher or the learner.

A practical approach

A curriculum needs to be practical. The matrix model is comprehensive, but it is also extremely complex, and it is difficult to visualise how student and practice teacher might cope with so many cells of learning to prepare for practice. The building block model, by contrast, is relatively easy to put into practice, and can be as precise as required. In part, this flexibility and user-friendliness is due to its structure and also because it is organised around skills, knowledge and values rather than around academic disciplines, as might be found in a curriculum taught in the classroom.

Sequential learning
In the description of the building block model it is evident that there is a notion of sequence in the way it is constructed, in that some items may need to be learned before others. Complex practice requires the possession of basic competence before more advanced skills, knowledge and values can be developed. This notion would provide a simple, linear model of sequencing, with one piece of learning following another. However, sequential learning may be too inflexible for social work practice. It may be more appropriate to conceive of the curriculum as a jigsaw, where a sense of order and place is apparent, but where it is possible to begin and build in many different ways, depending on our style. In this way non-linear sequences – patterns – can be used to complete the learning specified by a curriculum.

Planning and monitoring
Some elements of practice learning can be neglected, either because opportunities for learning about these are limited by the nature of placements, or because the nature of learning itself presents problems. With detailed curriculum units, each specifying the content of learning, it becomes possible to monitor the extent to which all required elements of learning are being incorporated into the learning of the placement. Where it is evident that one or more areas are not being addressed, the necessary learning opportunities can be introduced in a variety of different ways (see Chapter 6). Thus, student and practice teacher can be certain that the learning is comprehensive.

New approaches

The growth in importance of the competency model might seem to make the building block approach to the development of a practice curriculum redundant. If the competencies that students must achieve are specified at national level, what scope remains to the curriculum-builder for flexibility and creativity? At a general level this is true, since the competencies specify the *total* range of students' learning. However, the building block approach is useful to enable practice teachers (singly or as a group) to determine what range of skills and knowledge can be offered through the learning opportunities on a particular placement. If all the required competencies cannot be met through these learning experiences, on any given placement, it is incumbent on the practice teacher to seek out other suitable learning opportunities. Competencies alone do not provide a curriculum, primarily because they do not give the curriculum-user a sense of the relative weight, value and relationship of these competencies to each other; the building block approach provides the necessary relationships by clustering the content of the learning.

The structured learning model uses the building block approach to curriculum development because it is practical and readily understandable, it builds on existing good practices, and it is responsive to change and development. It has been adopted by some Diploma in Social Work programmes in the UK, notably by the South Yorkshire Consortium (South Yorkshire DipSW, 1993).

Approaching curriculum design

There is a considerable body of educational writing examining a variety of aspects of curriculum, including philosophy, content and implementation. It is not the intention here to review that material in detail, but rather to distil some key ingredients that might be helpful to practice teachers and students in the design of a curriculum for practice learning. Qualifying social work courses vary in the manner and degree to which the content of practice learning is defined by course-planners. Some practice teachers will be relatively autonomous in specifying and designing an individual curriculum for placements offered, others may have learning objectives specified or even a prescribed course curriculum to teach. Some may be bereft of any but the most superficial guidance.

Whichever of these situations exists, it is important for practice teachers and students to have at least a rudimentary understanding of curriculum design. In the absence of a defined practice curriculum, practice teachers will have to design their own. Where the practice teacher has the advantage of an 'off the shelf' curriculum, some interpretation and some 'customising' may be required to apply the curriculum to the practice context in which the practice teacher works. Moreover, no practice curriculum is fixed and static; each requires amendment and development to ensure its continued relevance and value. All of these processes require an appreciation of curriculum design. Similarly, students who wish to be fully involved in their own learning need to understand the way in which a curriculum structures the experience of learning on placement. Hence, it is helpful for both students and practice teachers to have some understanding of curriculum design.

Key principles

Before exploring some ways to design and develop a practice curriculum, it is necessary to consider in more detail some core aspects of the notion of curriculum, about which there is a great diversity of ideas; for example, there is an entire discipline of educational theory entitled 'curriculum studies' where fundamental concepts of curriculum are subject to analysis and debate. In curriculum studies, the focus of attention has moved away from early concerns such as the mechanics and technology of curriculum planning, as found in the seminal work of Tyler (1949). However, these are very much the concern of practice teachers and students.

As a discipline, curriculum studies now encompass wider debates about the politics and philosophy of knowledge and how these relate to the construction of a curriculum, including Illich's claim that traditional forms of education represent an invidious form of social control (1971), the influence of sexism on curriculum and the contribution of feminist thinking to curriculum design (Macdonald and Macdonald, 1988). The complexity, or apparent abstraction, of some of the recent debates about curriculum within educational theory need not distract teachers and students involved in learning about social work from considering the potential contribution and value of this branch of educational theory to the development of models of practice learning. For the moment, it is the practical – the *how to* – that is the principal concern, bearing in mind these radical critiques as a context within which the practice curriculum should be developed.

There is a deceptively simple, perhaps widely held, view that 'curriculum' is synonymous with 'syllabus' (the listing of subjects to be learned), and therefore a curriculum defines the *amount* of a discipline to be learned. For social work practice, this would consist of a listing of topics to be learned on a placement. This has been termed a *restricted curriculum*.

A restricted curriculum (sometimes called a formal curriculum) is limited primarily to defining the content or subject-matter to be taught, including a framework which places the material in a sequence, with the basic or more fundamental concepts learned first, allowing more complex ideas to be learned subsequently. This view of curriculum is well-expressed by Gagné, as quoted by Sockett:

> A curriculum is a series of content units arranged in such a way that the learning of each unit may be accomplished as a single act, provided that the capabilities described by specified prior units (in the sequence) have already been mastered by the learner. (Sockett, 1976, p. 23)

This is a teacher-focused curriculum, where the teacher is responsible for defining the content of each unit, for the sequence of learning and for the decision whether the student has made sufficient progress to move to the next unit of learning.

In comparison, an *extended curriculum* encompasses both the formal and the informal curriculum. The latter includes activities that occur outside formal teaching sessions: for example, these might include contacts between teachers and students or interactions between students in groups. These activities may be recreational, or focused on learning. The context and quality of an educational environment will affect the nature of learning that occurs in these situations. This type of curriculum does not specify solely the activities of the teacher or those of the learners, but includes both of these and allows for both teachers and students to help shape the informal curriculum. Coulshed describes an experiment to incorporate informal aspects of learning into the curriculum as part of a social work course:

> [Coulshed's institution], recognising that course processes can maximize learning opportunities and enhance the developmental experience of students, has purposely built these into the programme. (1989, p. 22)

She terms this the *process curriculum*. Students are required amongst other things to: evaluate the process of learning as they experience it, negotiate the content of teaching, engage in peer assessment, and develop personal learning plans. This maximises the students' learning. Coulshed presents a very broad approach to the idea of curriculum.

Another distinction, often made in curriculum studies, separates the curriculum which the teacher intends from the *hidden curriculum*. The term 'hidden curriculum' is used to refer to at least three distinct aspects of curriculum (Sockett, 1976):

- *the received lore of the student* – the knowledge that one generation of students transmits to the next: for example, about the quality of particular placements
- *what students actually learn as opposed to what their teacher*

thinks they are learning – in a practice tutorial session the explicit focus may be upon models of social work, but the student may really be learning that the practice teacher is poorly- or well-organised and can or cannot manage a constant stream of interruptions from clients

- *where the practice teacher has a hidden agenda* – as an example, in addition to knowledge about a theoretical approach, a student might also acquire the practice teacher's attitudes – hostile or committed – to this approach

There are other examples of secondary agendas, which may be consciously pursued by the practice teacher: for example, a student might be required to submit word-processed rather than hand-written assignments, in the expectation that the student will take the opportunity to learn word-processing skills.

Since there is no ideal type of practice curriculum, choices must be made about which elements of curriculum are used, and how far restricted, extended, or hidden elements are used positively.

> [Curriculum] is not a concept which has some existence outside and prior to human experience. Rather, it is a cultural construction. That is, it is not an abstract concept which has some existence outside of human experience. Rather, it is a way of organising a set of human educational practices. (Grundy, 1987, p. 5)

There are very many ways in which human experience might be organised for the purposes of learning. There is equally a diverse range of ways in which any curriculum might be interpreted and received by the learner. Individual students' experience of a curriculum will be affected by their personal biography (see Chapter 2). A programme might plan a curriculum, but it is difficult to know just how it will be received by individual students.

Constructing a practice curriculum

We wish to identify some principles drawn from educational literature to assist practice teachers and students in constructing a practice curriculum. It is not easy to select a few significant principles to guide busy practitioners from a complex and growing literature about curriculum studies, and much of the thinking about curriculum design is grounded in educational practice for schools, so the transformation to practice learning in social work is not straightforward. In the discussion that follows the principles selected are drawn from educationally orthodox ideas. These are not advanced uncritically, but familiarity with conventional wisdom is perhaps necessary before generating radical critiques.

Four essential constituents to be specified in a curriculum were first identified by Tyler, one of the earliest writers in the field (1949). These are:

- aims and objectives to be achieved through the curriculum
- subject-matter to be learned or content of the curriculum
- the kind of learning experiences to be provided
- evaluation of the extent to which the present aims and objectives have been achieved

Differing views have emerged about the importance of each of these elements and about how to begin to use those principles to design a curriculum. Kelly, for example, identifies three different focuses for planning and designing a curriculum (1989):

- the *objectives school*, where curriculum planning is a rational process that must be goal-directed, as exemplified by the work of Hirst (1969)
- the *content approach*, where primary importance is given to specifying the content of learning, as seen in the development of a National Curriculum for schools in the UK
- the *process model*, which uses principles about the ways

in which teachers act, as in the work of Stenhouse (1975)

The objectives school is represented by a diverse range of writers, united in the belief that the best way to design a curriculum is to begin by deciding upon the objectives to be achieved. This may seem the 'common sense' way to proceed, but exponents of this model may predicate curriculum design on a belief that the purpose of education is the transmission of knowledge. This is manifestly not the case in social work education, which is a highly complex process concerned with the acquisition of specific areas of knowledge, the attainment of competence in skill performance, and the incorporation of professional values. Professional education in social work cannot be reduced to the transmission of knowledge.

To plan a curriculum by reference to the content, it is necessary to have a very clear prescription about what should be learned. Given the diversity of views about the constituents of social work knowledge, skills and values, there may be considerable difficulty in using this approach to curriculum design. However, as greater centralised control is exercised over the curriculum, and learning is prescribed in more precise detail, this type of curriculum may become mandatory. It is possible to conceive of the development of a National Curriculum for social work in the UK.

However, it is within the third broad approach, the process model, that we wish to locate our approach to curriculum design as part of a structured learning model, because this approach allows us to recognise that neither education for social workers generally, nor the specifics of a curriculum for practice learning, are value-free. In whatever way the curriculum is constructed, it will represent and carry the ideological assumptions of those who framed it, and any attempt to purge the curriculum of ideological content is doomed. In these circumstances Stenhouse suggests what a curriculum might be:

> A curriculum is an attempt to communicate the essential principles and features of an educational proposal in such a

form that it is open to critical scrutiny and capable of effective translation into practice. (1975, p. 4)

The curriculum becomes one among many possible 'proposals' – where a proposal consists of an explicit statement of the underlying principles, objectives and content of the practice curriculum. This approach to curriculum permits us to have:

> our goals, purposes, intentions, aims as educators but frees us from the necessity of seeing these as extrinsic to the educational process and from the restrictions of having only one step-by-step route to their achievement. It allows us to have our content but frees us from the need to select this by reference to anything other than the principles inherent in our aims and purposes. (Kelly, 1989, p. 90)

This approach to the design of curriculum is particularly useful for the development of a social work practice curriculum. Practice teachers and students can frame their own curriculum according to the objectives that they themselves determine. Any practice curriculum designed in this manner would be judged within its own terms, that is, the extent to which the curriculum meets its own predetermined goals. Inevitably, these goals cannot be framed without reference to the overall course structure, and it would be undesirable if they could. We must consider how to apply these ideas in the construction and development of a curriculum for practice learning.

A practice curriculum: a do-it-yourself approach

At first glance, it may seem a very unwelcome task for a busy practice teacher to have to devise a practice curriculum. It is not easily avoided! Even where no explicit curriculum is written down, the practice teacher must operate a personal curriculum, however rudimentary, that specifies at least the opportunities for learning in a given placement. Where the programme has published a curriculum for all placements, interpretation and application to the particular placement setting is still necessary.

Whatever the nature of the task facing a practice teacher in relation to the practice curriculum, it does not have to be a solitary activity. Sharing curriculum development can be a rewarding joint enterprise with colleagues.

There is also an important role for students to play in this process. It will not always be possible for students to have such an active role in the design and formulation of the curriculum, as such tasks cannot be left until students arrive on placement. Students are consumers of curricula and, as such, have a vital role in the evaluation and review of the curriculum. This assists curriculum development for future students.

There are many ways of approaching curriculum design. The approach of this book is pragmatic and evolutionary. A good curriculum is not crafted in one event but evolves gradually over time, as it is tested and modified through evaluation based on use with students. For the busy practice teacher and student, a curriculum designed for practice learning must effectively and efficiently organise materials and be directly applicable to their practice context. Curriculum design can be compared to the process of designing and constructing a building such as a house (Sockett, 1976). Houses are built in varied styles and they can be modified over time by removing features or adding extensions. Although a house is built to a plan, it is often difficult to visualise life in a house until you take up residence. So it is with a practice curriculum; it is difficult to know if the paper version works until it has been tested in practice.

An approach to designing your own curriculum is suggested. This employs a series of stages, and at each stage a question is asked to promote the framing of a part of a practice curriculum. Designing a curriculum need not be a linear process, so that different parts can be developed at various times and in differing ways.

Step 1   Defining aims – the proposal

What am I attempting to achieve through this curriculum?
The curriculum proposal (the descriptive overview of the curriculum) makes explicit the purpose of the curriculum and contains a clear specification of the aims and objectives. Decisions must be made about the proximity of goals to be achieved, distinguishing the short-term from the long-term. These statements about the curriculum need to be framed in terms which recognise that alternative curricula could address the area of learning mapped out; no particular curriculum is definitive in form, structure, or content. Curriculum-builders should also make explicit the value premises that underpin the curriculum, even if it is problematic to encapsulate these ideas in brief statements.

In framing the proposal, the curriculum authors must recognise that the function of a curriculum for practice learning is not merely the transmission of knowledge, but it must offer the learner the opportunity for guided development through a range of experiences. From these experiences, learners will make their own synthesis and create their own understandings, and these will be unique for each individual. Most curricula will be framed by practice teachers in advance of student placements. Choice and flexibility can be incorporated within the curriculum, and the relationship between a practice curriculum and other component parts of students' learning need to be specified.

Step 2   Identifying teaching content

What is the student to learn – in detail?
A good place to start for experienced practice teachers is to write down the areas of learning that have previously been offered on placement. This task may be less easy for the novice practice teacher, and it becomes more a question of specifying the areas that you hope to offer. Having listed these areas of learning, search for themes. How can what may seem at first to be a very disparate list of areas of learning be categorised and grouped into broad themes? At this point, curriculum-building can be a cre-

ative process, since there are many ways of organising the material into broad categories. As well as deciding on the type of categories, it is essential to fix their number. External constraints imposed by the course may suggest that components of learning (units, in the terminology adopted here) should be divided according to a certain pattern. To allow for ease of use, it is desirable not to have too many broad units or major themes; we suggest between two and six units of learning for a placement.

Once a broad organising structure exists, the location of smaller packages of learning (modules, in the terminology adopted here) can be determined. Some aspects of learning may obviously belong under one unit, and others may relate to several. In more difficult cases, some may not fit into any unit at all. This may suggest that the unit groups need amending, or that the modules need to be redesigned, or that some modules need to be taught elsewhere, or rejected altogether because they do not fit within the aims of the curriculum. This process of determining the overall shape and content of the curriculum, by bringing together a series of modules and units, is illuminating, since it helps to distinguish the more important from the less important elements of practice learning.

In developing the curriculum content, there is inevitably a compromise between national requirements, as specified by regulating bodies, and the notions of practice defined at the local programme or individual level. These tensions can promote dialogue about the content and interpretation of the curriculum. Nevertheless, the scope of the curriculum needs to be limited in some way (for instance, by delineating the knowledge, skills and values to be addressed). There is an understandable desire to include too much in a curriculum, but it is to be resisted.

Step 3   Sequencing

Does the student have to approach the curriculum in any particular order?
Decisions have to made about whether the curriculum includes a notion of sequence. Do some of the units or

modules require completion before the student can obtain maximum learning benefit from others? For example,
does some of the learning material contain fundamental
principles or core knowledge? If so, the curriculum document must specify these elements and help to ensure that
the student studies these components before moving on
to other sections of greater complexity. Even if the material
in the curriculum imposes no required sequence of learning,
it is still necessary to decide if students are to be given
an unfettered choice about how they approach the curriculum. Also, other factors – such as availability of work –
may constrain the sequence of progress through the curriculum. As far as possible, it is helpful for teacher and
learner if these constraints can be specified at the outset.

Step 4   Devising methods and strategies of learning

*What methods of learning are to be employed in delivering the
curriculum?*
A tremendous range of learning opportunities are available on placement and the practice curriculum may be
taught using a variety of methods. Questions to be considered by practice teachers and students are:

- will a broad range of methods to promote learning be
  used or will there be a concentration upon a few methods?
- why have the particular methods been chosen?
- do the methods used reinforce the content of the
  curriculum?

These themes will be considered further in Chapter 6, as
part of the elaboration of a structured learning model.

Step 5   Using examination methods

How should a student's competence to practise be measured?
Just as with content and methods there are considerable
choices to be made about the way in which the curriculum is examined, so the questions to be posed are similar to those in the previous section:

- how broad is the range of approaches to be used to examine competence in the curriculum?
- why have the particular approaches been chosen?
- do these approaches fit with the content and methods of teaching, and do the modes of examination reinforce the learning?

Again, these themes will be considered further in Chapter 7 as part of the structured learning model.

Step 6   Publication

How is the curriculum to be made available to students and practice teachers?
To be useful to students and teachers alike, a curriculum must be available in writing. Something that exists only in the curriculum-builders' minds cannot be easily grasped by others, nor can it be modified and developed in response to the comments of others. It is not explicit and available, and therefore it breaches ethical standards about open educational practices.

Consideration must be given to the form, layout and presentation of the curriculum as these presentational factors can greatly influence colleagues' abilities to use the curriculum with ease. Loose-leaf formats which allow easy modification and replacement of material are very useful. A valuable test to apply about the quality of presentation is to ask:

- is the material presented in a simple, engaging manner, so that a student with no prior knowledge can grasp quickly the essential features of the curriculum?

Step 7   Review and evaluation

How can the curriculum be modified in the light of experience?
Mechanisms to review the curriculum need to be specified as an integral part of the curriculum itself. The extent to which the curriculum meets the agreed objectives through

its content, methods of learning and examination processes needs careful consideration by all those who use
the curriculum to prevent it from becoming less and less
relevant.

The implementation of a practice learning curriculum
needs to be carefully evaluated and monitored, so that it
can adapt to the experiences of students and practice
teachers. Evaluation of the curriculum need not be a single
event towards the end of the placement. It can be a process
incorporated into the active use of a curriculum, with
regular consideration given to its development.

Step 8   Summary

When all of these questions have been considered, the
overall shape of the practice curriculum should become
clear. It can then be written as a document containing
the following elements:

- the proposal (the aims, objectives and purpose of the
  curriculum)
- content of learning
- sequence or patterns of learning
- strategies for learning
- modes of examining competence
- publication
- process for review and evaluation

Using a curriculum

For the student and the practice teacher, the acid test of
the value of a practice curriculum is through application
to practice on placement. Adopting a practice curriculum eases the difficulties of identifying the nature of learning to be achieved during different placements on the
same course. It becomes more feasible to identify areas
of learning that can occur on one placement, allowing
other more complex skills, knowledge and values to be
developed in subsequent placements. The use of a cur-

riculum makes explicit choices that would otherwise be hidden. For these key reasons the development and use of an explicit practice curriculum is incorporated into the structured learning model.

However, there are also dangers in using a practice curriculum. If applied without concern for the unique learning needs of each student, it can become a corset and constrain the opportunities for learning. It provides a structure to help and promote learning but should not be used uncritically. Students and practice teachers can work together to ensure that expectations are shared about how the curriculum will be used to structure learning on the placement. To what extent will practice experiences be related to the curriculum? Alternatively, to what extent will the curriculum be used to make sense of practice experiences? If a practice curriculum is to be used successfully, it will become a regular feature of the discussions between practice teacher and student, and form the backbone of the placement.

6

Methods of Learning

Summary

Many different ways of promoting learning on placements
are available to students and practice teachers. In this
chapter an important context for learning, the 'practice
tutorial', is explored as a preliminary to considering some
of the different methods of learning that can be used on
placement. Some principles for choosing which method
to use are suggested. Finally, four broadly defined methods of learning are considered: modelling; learning by
enactment; simulation and learning; and learning from
published materials. Guidance on the use of these methods of learning is presented.

The practice tutorial: a context for learning

There are very many different methods of learning that
can be used by practice teachers and students on placements. There are choices to be made by both practice
teacher and student; practice teachers must decide which
learning possibilities are practical, and students must decide what methods of learning they would like to use on
placement. From a dialogue between students and practice teachers about the range of possibilities and the student's preferences, a range of different methods of learning
can be selected for use on the placement. However, there
is one context for learning, the practice tutorial, which

needs consideration before it is possible to explore some of the different methods of learning on placement and the circumstances in which these might be used.

The practice tutorial has been a linchpin for promoting social work students' learning on placement (the tutorial has been known by a variety of names: supervision session, practice teaching session, practice supervision). A 'practice tutorial' is a meeting between student and practice teacher to enable the student's practice learning. It is formal to the extent that it is pre-planned, with an agenda. It commonly takes place at weekly intervals. Using the terminology *practice tutorial* firmly locates this event within the orbit of teaching, by using language conventionally associated with learning rather than with the managerial connotations of *supervision*. The term 'tutorial' usually brings to mind a particular context of teaching, where a student and teacher meet in face to face discussion, and focus upon the student's learning. Using 'practice' signifies two aspects: the location (the tutorial occurs in a practice agency) and the content (the subject matter of the tutorial is social work practice).

Some of other terms, such as 'practice supervision', resonate with other processes in social work, i.e. the *supervision* given by a manager to a social work practitioner. Aspects of this supervision may include learning, but the primary focus in the meeting between a social worker and a manager is to ensure managerial accountability for the practitioner's work. Terms which describe managerial processes can cause confusion about the function of meetings between practice teachers and students.

There is not a lot of evidence from research to guide us, but the practice tutorial appears to have been the dominant mode of learning, at least until recently. The practice tutorial has most often been used as a forum for discussing intended work with particular clients, and reviewing this work. Students undertake this work independently, and students' self-reports about the results have been analysed in subsequent practice tutorials. This approach to learning has much to commend it, except when it is used to the exclusion of other methods. It is possible that the practice tutorial is developing in more creative ways; this is significant, because the use made by both student and practice teacher of the practice tutorial will greatly affect the quality of learning on the placement. A key factor in the way the practice tutorial is used will be the personal biographies of both student and practice teacher (see Chapter 2).

The practice tutorial has several functions, which have been variously described over time. This conceptualisation draws particularly upon the work of Reynolds and Kadushin (Reynolds, 1942; Kadushin, 1973). From their writings, some of the most important functions of the practice tutorial can be identified:

- *Educative function*
  The practice tutorial is the focus for communications between practice teachers and students; it is the opportunity to discuss and plan the student's work and to provide guidance and evaluation about the student's performance. All elements of the educative process find legitimate expression within the practice tutorial.

- *Pastoral function*
  In the academic world, tutors have long been used to discussing students' personal difficulties affecting the process of learning. Similarly, practice teachers have a long history of providing such help and support to students. Some practice teachers, when teaching students in agencies, have pathologised students on placement, to the extent that they have been expected to possess and reveal personal difficulties to the practice teacher. In this way the student could pass through the psychological pain barrier necessary to become a qualified social worker. Whilst these beliefs and practices no longer characterise the learning experience of students, there may be residual fears among some students that this could be a part of the tutorial relationship. Students need to control the pastoral aspect of the practice tutorial and must be enabled to ask for help if and when needed.

- *Managerial function*
  The practice teacher has a responsibility to the agency's

clients to ensure that they receive an acceptable level of service from students on placement. This is not normally a problem; indeed, students may well provide a higher level of service to clients than the agency's workers simply because they have more time. It is not just the clients who need to receive a good service, so should students. It is part of the function of the practice teacher to manage the amount and type of work that students perform on behalf of the agency; for example, students should not have to undertake work that is too difficult or complex for their current abilities. These managerial functions should not dominate the practice teacher to the exclusion of the students learning needs.

- *Administrative function*
  The practice tutorial is a good opportunity to make sure that all the administrative arrangements for the placement run smoothly – that the student has access to all the necessary administrative functions the agency provides, and that the administrative requirements associated with the placement are completed satisfactorily.

The 'practice tutorial' is taken to mean a series of regular planned meetings, most usually on a weekly basis, between practice teacher and student. Frequently, these will involve only one practice teacher and one student. This structure provides a highly individualised approach to learning (this is becoming something of a rarity within higher education generally in the UK as the system expands to accommodate increased numbers of students). Practice teachers and students are increasingly experimenting with other forms of practice tutorial; for example, group tutorials where one practice teacher works with several students to facilitate learning. Group tutorials can be set up on a reciprocal basis with other practice teachers in the same or different agencies, to allow students to benefit from each other's experiences and the expertise of different practitioners. Practice teachers have attempted to provide too much of the learning experience for students, and sharing responsibility for practice tutorials can reduce students' reliance upon a single practice teacher.

It is also possible for a group of practice teachers to meet with a group of students. This type of tutorial can be extremely useful at key points in the placement when students have common experiences that benefit from shared discussion: for example, consideration of a common practice theme, such as assessment, where discussion in a group setting can provide a rich and diverse forum for learning. Many other forms of practice tutorial are possible: for example, tandem arrangements where two practice teachers work jointly with one student. Such arrangements are especially beneficial to the novice practice teacher.

Practice tutorials provide an important opportunity for students and practice teachers to share the responsibilities of promoting the student's learning. As with any meeting, the function and purpose of the tutorial needs to be explicit, clear and agreed by all participants. To achieve these objectives, a mutually agreed agenda is a helpful first step, especially if combined with some mechanism to ensure that all items are given a reasonable allocation of available time. Also, there needs to be some way to record the content of discussion and any decisions made. Various possibilities exist to help make the recording fair. It can, for example, be a joint task shared in alternate sessions, between practice teacher and student. Whatever structures are adopted to help the practice tutorial work well, it is necessary to create a climate where the student feels able to contribute and participate. If students are not able to raise their concerns in a practice tutorial, it is not operating satisfactorily.

Practice tutorials require the development of many skills if practice teacher and student are to make the best use of this context for learning. Above all else, the practice teacher needs to develop the skill of giving an appraisal of the student's practice performance, remembering how easy it is to snuff out developing competence by over-robust or careless appraisal. Some suggestions for giving feedback on performance are given below:

The student's behaviour

Focus the comments on the student's behaviour, rather than attributes of the student's personality. It is important to refer to what a person is rather than what you imagine they are. Observations are always to be preferred to inferences. For example, commenting upon a section of an observed interview a practice teacher might say:

Focus on behaviour

'It was a good idea to point out the consequences to the client. What you had to say came over as very serious, and I think it would have helped to inject some humour into it.'
rather than
'You seemed to be rather humourless.'

Specific behaviours

Select specific behaviours exhibited by the student for comment rather than more generalised traits, for example:

Specific behaviours

'She responded by looking up at you directly when you held her hand and that helped her to start talking with you.'
rather than
'You've got a good way with depressed people.'

Sharing ideas and information

The comments made to the student should focus on the sharing of ideas and information, rather than on giving advice (although there are, of course, some situations where advice must be given). In general, this is more valuable to the learner. It leaves the student free to decide for themselves how to use these ideas. It is more valuable to explore alternatives, rather than to offer answers or solutions:

Sharing of ideas

'I was interested that you decided to tell him about a similar experience which happened to you, because I wasn't sure he appreciated it. Why did you decide to do that?'
rather than
'You shouldn't have told him about what happened to you. It's a bad idea to disclose your own experiences and you should have let him work it out for himself.'

Enhancing the student's learning

Remember that the purpose of providing comments about performance is to enhance the student's learning. Therefore, the focus should be on the comments that will have value for the student, not on the 'sense of release' it may provide for the person giving the feedback:

Enhance learning

'Although it was helpful to bring the subject up, I think she got angry because she felt you treated her like a child when you were telling her what to do. Do you think that's the reason? When you tell me

what to do that's how I feel.'
rather than
'Quite frankly I'm not surprised she got angry with
you – I've been wanting to say the same thing for
ages.'

Positive improvement and change

It is helpful to put comments about behaviour in a framework of being 'more' or 'less' helpful rather than in terms
of being 'either/or'. It is also helpful if comments concentrate upon suggestions for positive improvement and
change if necessary:

What is more or less helpful

'I thought it was helpful the way you came into the
room and looked directly at him. I think it would
have been even more helpful to have walked straight
in, without hesitating at the doorway – what do you
think?'
rather than
'You shouldn't have hesitated at the doorway.'

Adapted from Johnson (1993) and Wilkinson and Canter (1982).

Feedback is often categorised as being either negative or
positive – positive feedback indicating that a task has been
performed well, negative feedback indicating that the task
was not performed satisfactorily and if repeated the task
needs to be undertaken differently. This categorisation is
unsatisfactory because it can suggest that there is something undesirable about the feedback itself, in the case
of negative feedback. This need not be the case, as all
feedback can be useful to the person receiving the feed-

back if it is given helpfully. For this reason an alternative categorisation is proposed: *affirming feedback* where the giver is indicating their agreement with the way a task was performed; *challenging feedback* where the giver wishes to encourage the receiver to consider alternative approaches.

On placement, students need to receive regular feedback, both *affirming* and *challenging* to help them learn. There is perhaps a tendency to provide insufficient affirming feedback in many learning situations – possibly we all need to remind ourselves that people learn best from encouragement.

Using and developing these methods of feedback in the practice tutorial will help to ensure high quality practice learning. No doubt, practice teachers and students would wish to add to these guiding principles and build a greater repertoire of scripts.

Methods of learning

The *structured learning model* encourages the use of a wide range of methods of learning, especially when these are selected according to certain principles. Examples of the diverse teaching and learning methods used by practice teachers and students is listed below:

SOME METHODS OF LEARNING ON PLACEMENT
- direct work with clients
- self-analysis of material captured on video or audio tape
- observation of practice
- reading prepared texts
- formal simulations
- teaching exercises
- group learning techniques
- diagrams and graphics
- games
- reading material
- pre-recorded video.

Sawdon (1985) has used six categories of *Action Technique* to describe the range of teaching methods available. With such a range of methods available to enable learning, choosing the most valuable or useful for a given learning task is by no means easy. It does not have to be a random choice, and there are certain principles that help to determine which method of learning is most appropriate. Whatever method is decided, practice teachers and students can jointly negotiate and select the method of learning used in any particular instance. This is itself a valuable exercise. Some initial factors to be taken into account when selecting methods of learning are:

- *The range of technical resources available* – there is little point wishing to use video recordings of students' work, or CD ROM interactive learning packages if the equipment and facilities are not readily available.
- Most methods of learning require that teachers are familiar with *key principles* – there is nothing to prevent teacher and student jointly approaching a new method of learning. However, the quality of learning for the student may be adversely affected.

A complex range of factors needs to be considered for the practice teacher and student to decide which method of learning to use to help develop a particular skill, acquire an area of knowledge, or address a question of social work values. The most important are:

- The influence of socially structured difference on the student's personal biography, and the implications that this might have for the student's approach to learning.
- The student's preferred learning strategies and how these relate to any proposed methods of learning (student and practice teacher may also have an agreement that different methods of learning will be used to expand the student's preferred learning strategies during the placement).
- The particular form of practice curriculum may create restrictions on the type of learning methods that can be used.

- Finally, there are a range of guiding principles that can be used to help students and practice teachers when choosing a practice method (see below).

All of these factors need to be considered when selecting a method of learning in any given circumstance. Let us consider the final element in this equation (the others relate to earlier chapters), the principles involved in selecting a practice method. These principles form a part of the structured learning model.

Harmony

There needs to be *harmony* between the method of learning selected and the learning task itself. This occurs where the method of learning and the task to be learned are in accord. We can illustrate this principle with a musical analogy:

> It is not possible to learn how to play the cello by studying books alone. Musical theory can be learned without reference to any instrument, but to accomplish the practical skill of playing the cello, it is necessary to learn by practice on the instrument itself.

In this analogy there is harmony between the method of learning and the skill to be learned, because the required skill can be acquired through the method selected. Learning to play the cello by books alone is not harmonious because of the mismatch between the nature of the skill to be learned and the method of learning. Similarly, for social work practice, there should be harmony between the method of learning and the area of practice learning in question.

Effectiveness

Methods of learning must also be *effective*. Placements have time limits, which constrain the opportunity for students to learn about practice, so it is important to make best use of a range of learning opportunities. As far as possible, students should have the opportunity to accelerate their learning (Doel, 1988). *Effectiveness* of learning is a complex notion, not simply a question of measuring a given quantity of learning as plotted against the time invested by the student to produce a desired learning outcome. *Effective learning* must also take account of the *quality* of learning. High quality learning is difficult to define, but can be measured through indicators such as the learner's appraisal of the impact of any learning opportunity, the degree of comprehension, the likelihood of retention, and the potential for influencing practice.

Selecting a method of learning involves difficult judgements, and we have to be prepared for the fact that 'effectiveness' may not be quantifiable until after the completion of the practice learning.

Efficiency

Teaching on placements is frequently is one-to-one. This is a luxurious ratio compared to many other teacher–learner situations, and it is important for practice teachers to be mindful of the need to teach *efficiently*, to think carefully about how they use the time available for promoting and enabling learning. For example, tasks should not be undertaken as joint face to face activities if they can be performed equally well by the student outside of the practice tutorial, perhaps involving other colleagues.

Linkage to curriculum

The adoption and use of an explicit practice curriculum facilitates greater systematisation and creativity in the use of methods of learning. Using a practice curriculum allows pre-planning and selection of particular learning methods, and these can be linked to specific modules or units of the curriculum, which allows a wide variety of learning methods to be incorporated into the placement. This is an important principle, because it encourages different learning opportunities which can stretch the student's competence and enhance their repertoire of strategies for learning. Balancing the use of different approaches is made easier within the framework of an explicit curriculum where student choice can be accommodated more effectively.

Selecting a method

To choose which method to use to promote practice learning, practice teachers and students need to balance each of these four guiding principles. It is not easy, because one principle may suggest one method whilst another is indicated by another principle. It is helpful if practice teachers and students can jointly discuss and consider the factors governing the selection of different methods of learning.

Major methods of promoting learning on placement

It has already been suggested that there are a variety of methods to promote learning on placement. Having considered some principles that can be used to guide the choice of methods, let us turn our attention to the methods themselves and how these might be used on placement. It is not possible to review the use of all methods of learning at the disposal of practice teachers and students. However, it is possible to categorise these methods into four different groups, and to consider some advantages and disadvantages of each category. It is also possible to offer some guidelines about the use of some methods of learning. A successful and balanced placement ought to contain a significant number of these methods, and a full implementation of the structured learning model would employ methods from each of these categories during a placement.

Learning by modelling
Modelling, is a process of learning by observing an experienced practitioner complete a skill and then imitating the practitioner's behaviour. This process enables us to learn many very complex behaviours, as Hudson and Macdonald comment:

> Modelling accounts for the acquisition of a vast range of very different behaviours: skills simple and complex, from washing dishes to brain surgery, from social good manners to conducting a philosophical debate. (1986, p. 41)

If modelling can enable learning about these tasks, why not social work? If social work students do not see other practitioners in action, how can they begin to develop their own competent approach to practice? Social work entails a complex range of skills, knowledge and values, which are not easily defined, delineated and written into authoritative instruction manuals. Observing others in practice provides raw material, from which the novice can develop their own approach. Students who observe practitioners working with clients have the opportunity to see role models for their own practice.

In the past, some practitioners have been reluctant to use this method of learning. The justifications advanced for not enabling learning in this way have been both educational and ethical. The educational arguments rest on two principles: a desire to allow students to develop their own style; and a recognition that many different and valid approaches to social work exist. When combined, these two principles have led many practice teachers to be reluctant to offer themselves as role models to students, because this might imply that their approach to practice is the best and therefore ought to be adopted by students. Such arguments have inhibited practice teachers from giving opportunities to students to observe practice. These views may be less dominant than they once were, but they have been influential.

Second, turning to ethical considerations, social work practice has too long been a relatively private activity. What occurs between the practitioner and client has been regarded by many social workers as sacrosanct. No doubt, there are situations where it is undesirable to have students' observe a practice teacher's work with a client. However, this is rarely considered to be the case in residential and group practice, and less so in field work settings, as it is currently developing in local authorities in Britain. In these situations, the content of practice is rarely solely confidential between client and social worker. Whatever the reality of practice, the influence of an *idealised* notion of preserving the clients' confidences remains strong.

For some practitioners, there also remain residual doubts about the desirability of allowing another person to be present during the interchange between social worker and client, for fear of having a detrimental effect on the work. Such worries and fears need to be addressed both for clients and workers. It is not yet universally accepted that practice ought to be open, but there are strong currents that encourage social workers to develop a greater openness in practice with clients. The greater involvement of social work students in the work of colleagues may have a significant effect on making the content of social work more accessible.

How can students best be helped to learn from modelling? They may observe experienced colleagues' practice in a variety of different ways. A common image of observing practice is one of the student sitting quietly in the corner of the room, taking no part in the proceedings, but this is only one of many possible approaches. Students do not necessarily have to be present in the room during an interview, since audio and video tape can be used to 'capture' examples of colleagues' work. Some practice teachers will be fortunate and will have access to sophisticated observation systems, one-way mirrors and video suites. In some settings, especially group care, there are many opportunities for students to observe colleagues in a natural way, as part of everyday work.

Whichever approach is used to provide opportunities for student observation of practice, students need to develop the potential for learning which modelling presents. The student needs to know what is expected of them, and to be able to observe relevant aspects of practice. Students cannot be expected to be proficient in the complex skills of social work practice without the chance to rehearse them. Students need to recognise that observations must be focused around a particular theme, otherwise their analysis will be too diffuse. Practice teacher and student should agree the aspects of practice to be observed during any interaction and devise the criteria for making judgements about the quality of observed practice. When the student is familiar with this method in principle, it can be used. To guide students and practice teachers a series of steps to use modelling effectively are suggested below:

Modelling – a suggested approach

- Step one: select a subject for observation – colleague or practice teacher and client.
- Step two: select the technology – live observation in the same room, video recording, audio recording, observation behind a hidden mirror, etc.
- Step three: agree the aspect of practice to be observed – e.g. skills in demonstrating empathy, engaging a client, undertaking a problem scan, etc.
- Step four: through joint discussion, agree criteria of good practice for the skills to be used, the student will use these criteria to make judgements about the quality of practice observed (this list should be relatively brief, otherwise the student will have too much to look out for).
- Step five: select a mode of presenting the student's observations – by discussion in the practice tutorial, by written analysis, etc.
- Step six: the student has an opportunity to practise the skill with a client: a method of recording the practice is necessary; e.g. student self-report, audio tape, video tape, observation by the practice teacher, etc.
- Step seven: discussion and evaluation in a practice tutorial of the effectiveness of this example of learning by modelling.

During the course of a placement, it is helpful for students to have opportunities to observe several different colleagues in practice; if a student only observes the practice teacher, the student's learning will be greatly restricted. It is desirable for students to observe practitioners of different 'races' and gender, and practitioners who can provide diversity in the approaches and styles of practice to be observed.

Learning by enactment
Learning by doing has generally been the most significant way in which social work students have learned about practice, and it is likely that this method of learning will continue to keep its dominance in student learning on placement. In this method, students are given people to work with (users of the agency), and they learn by doing social work. It is a very valuable method of learning, but the danger for both students and clients lies in overuse or incautious use. As a method of learning it can present extremely creative challenges, or it may be reduced to the mundane by merely exposing students to work with clients with little attempt to structure the experience of learning. We wish to propose some guidelines for how this method may be effectively used. These consist of three stages in the use of this method:

Preparation. Before any direct work with clients, students need adequate preparation for the task that they are going to undertake. This might entail using some other approaches before the student gets live experience of clients: for example, a student with little experience of the role of being a social worker or knowledge of interview skills may need some rehearsal through simulated practice before having contact with clients (see below). Preparation might also consist of setting the student some assignments, for example to find out about the experience of being a client from published sources, such as Davies (1984a) and Chinnery (1990). Most important, students will require the opportunity to discuss their concerns and to plan their work with the client through the practice tutorial.

The performance. A traditional approach to learning by enactment would be for the practice teacher and student to discuss the piece of work in a practice tutorial and for the student independently to complete the face to face work with the client. This can place the student in a vulnerable and unsupported position. Just because the student is learning by *working* with clients directly it does not follow that the student must, or ought to, work alone. It is possible for the practice teacher and student to work together by conducting interviews jointly, if there is a prior agreement about the role and function that the student will undertake during the interview. In these circumstances, a practice teacher can provide the student with a protected experience of direct work with clients. Only when students are ready need they work independently. A disadvantage with this method of working is the amount of practice teacher time taken.

Example – linking modelling and enactment

A student with a moderate amount of experience in group care practice joins a field work agency. The student has little experience of conducting interviews and describes themselves as lacking confidence in this area of work. The practice teacher's team arrange for the student to observe several social workers conducting interviews with clients – having first ident-ified key aspects of practice to observe. After several of these interviews where the student observes a prac-tising social worker, the practice teacher selects a case and agrees with the student that they will conduct the work jointly. The student gradually assumes in-creased responsibility for the case, to the extent that the student feels confident to manage the work. This might entail two or three visits to the client where both student and practice teacher interview the client. At each subsequent interview the student may take greater responsibility for conducting the interview.

The approach to practice learning in the example can be developed in sophisticated ways, and has become known as 'live supervision'. This approach adds much to the *learning by doing* method. In live supervision approaches to learning the practice teacher is in the same room as the student and client, participating in the interview and also advising the student about their performance. Clearly, this requires considerable skill on the part of the practice teacher. Evans (1987) suggests that there are four advantages to using this approach:

1. That the practice teacher can have increased confidence in the student's assessment opinions.
2. Practice teachers can ensure that an agency's policies and any legal requirements are maintained.
3. The practice teacher has direct access to and acquaintance with the student's practice style. This is invaluable in subsequent practice tutorials and enables the practice teacher to make more helpful comments and better analyses than would otherwise have been possible.
4. Practice teachers are able to gain credibility with students by offering concrete suggestions that work.

Of these, the most important for promoting student learning is the direct access afforded the practice teacher and the opportunity this offers for immediate feedback to the student. Skilled practice teachers can also provide advice to students about the conduct of the interview during the interview itself. An alternative valuable technique is to create a five or ten minute break during the interview to provide the opportunity to discuss the process of the interview. As Toussaint and colleagues (1989) state:

> 'Time out' for discussion between Practice Teacher and Student may need to take place in the presence of the client. The client will certainly speak up if you've got the wrong end of the stick. (1989, p. 10)

There are a great many possibilities to be explored by practice teachers and students through using modes of learning such as live supervision as part of the process of

learning by enactment. Some practice teachers will be fortunate to have advanced technological aids: e.g. rooms
with one way mirrors, or direct methods of advising students
such as the 'bug in the ear' to provide immediate comment and guidance. All this is possible without the practice teacher being in the same room as the student. These
approaches require practice and planning and, ideally,
advice from experienced colleagues who have used such
methods. However, we should remind ourselves that the
various technological devices are not required to develop
'live supervision' as part of learning by doing.

Review. After the face to face contact with the client, the
student needs an opportunity to reflect upon and review
their performance and to identify key elements of learning. This can be done in a variety of ways, and students
can be encouraged to reflect upon their own performance either independently, with a student led group of
peers in the same agency, through the tutorial process,
or by structured exercises. These might consist of asking
the student to evaluate a particular element of the face
to face work. Ideally, this is best if agreed with the student
in advance of the work being completed. The student is
then ready to repeat the process with the next piece of
work.

Learning by enactment may be seen by some as the
only legitimate form of learning on placement because it
is 'real work' with 'real people'. The value of *learning by
doing* is enormous, but only as a part of a package of
learning methods. Various technologies are also available
to help practice teacher and student with learning by
enactment. The most easily available, is the audio tape
recorder, which allows the practice teacher and student
to have an accurate record of the interview for analysis
and discussion. Accessible video recording technology is
now compact enough to be taken and used for interviews
with clients in any setting. This has the distinct advantage over audio tape of providing a visual record of the
interview, which adds an extra dimension to possibilities
for learning and analysis. Both of these technologies are

now available to most social work agencies, at least on a limited basis. Less likely to be so readily available is the interview room which includes a one way screen – this can be used in conjunction with video or audio recording. Wherever such technologies are available, students must have the opportunity to become proficient through rehearsal before attempting to use them with clients, and they need to handle competently the ethical issues that arise from each of these methods. For example, where the content of interviews are to be recorded, it is essential that the prior (written?) agreement of the client is obtained and adequate measures taken to ensure that the recordings are stored safely and eventually disposed of carefully. People who are on videotape should know the purposes for which the tape is being used, who will have access to it, and how it will be disposed of.

Learning by simulation
The idea of using simulation is not new. Meinert (1972) has reviewed possible applications of simulation in social work education. The current use of simulation among practice teachers is probably not very high, though it is difficult to estimate with any confidence. In the absence of hard evidence, we know all too little of the methods and content actually used by practice teachers with students (Shardlow and Doel, 1992a). Simulation methods in practice learning encompass any approach where students learn though encounters with materials that represent reality. Simulation methods are an essential part of the *simulated learning model*. They have distinct advantages, as Arkava and Brennen comment:

> Everyone recognises the advantages of the Link Trainer for pilot training in which the student 'manoeuvres' a stationary machine that can be programmed for problems encountered in takeoffs, actual flights, or landings. (1976, p. 12)

The metaphor of the flight simulator is a common image, when thinking of learning through simulation. However, simulation in social work does not require the same level of technology as in pilot training and can require only modest resources such as a tape recorder, written exercises, or a workbook (Doel and Shardlow, 1993). Of course, very elaborate machinery can be used, and in the future there may be a greater use of interactive learning programmes based upon CD ROM technologies. For most practice teachers and students at present only lower levels of technology are likely to be available.

What are the advantages of simulation in practice learning? Arkava and Brennen (1976) were more impressed with the potential of simulation for standardising assessments of social work students (through measuring students responses to identical situations), than in the potential of simulation for learning. Whilst this is an attractive model for examination, it may be prudent to develop its use in learning before developing examination applications. Some of the advantages of simulation methods of practice learning are:

- *Protection for clients*
  Learning by simulation can protect clients from inexperienced practitioners. For example, the student with minimal experience of interviewing clients can practice in a 'role rehearsal simulation' (e.g. enacting an interview between student and client either with another student or with practice teachers simulating the role of the client). Students can derive confidence from rehearsal before actual live performance with clients. Rehearsal presents an opportunity to try out various different strategies and to see how these might be received. Also, the rehearsal can be interrupted, if desired, to provide advice to the student about how to conduct the interview. This permits the student to modify their approach or experiment with different strategies during the course of a practice interview. Before engaging in actual direct work with clients, students can be well prepared if they have observed other practitioners working with clients and also engaged in some simulation to gain experience of the problems themselves.

- *Timing of learning*
Simulations present the practice teacher and student with a vehicle to control the timing and scope of learning. Where student learning is, almost exclusively, tied to experiences gained in direct practice with clients, the nature and content of learning is inevitably constrained by the range of experience presented by the group of clients that the student works with. This presents some problems in ensuring that all the requirements of a practice curriculum are delivered. There may be areas of work essential to the students' future practice that do not always occur on a placement (for example some placements provide little opportunity to work with clients). Sometimes practice teachers and learners have adopted a fatalistic view that the unpredictability of practice learning is just a natural phenomenon over which we have little control and about which nothing can be done (Doel, 1990).

However, the quality of social work education cannot be satisfactory if there are wide gaps in students' experience. Consider the following analogy; as patients, we would be unhappy about qualified medical practitioners who indicated that they knew nothing about a common diseases because it had not figured in their training! Likewise, clients have the right to expect that social workers will have comprehensive knowledge and experience to enable them to provide a high quality service. Simulation can provide a very valuable method of learning to overcome gaps in a student's experience. It is also an important method in its own right and should not merely be used to compensate for the lack of other suitable methods.

- *An opportunity to rehearse dangerous situations*
Simulation presents for the social work student, as for the airline pilot, the opportunity to rehearse situations which are unlikely to happen but which need preparation in advance. The airline pilot may never have to control a plane during a crash, yet it is essential that the pilot is trained in advance how to deal with emergencies should a crash ever occur. So it is with

the social worker, who needs preparation on how to deal with difficult or dangerous situations, such as those involving verbally abusive or physically aggressive clients. Students cannot be expected to deal with these situations on the basis of 'common sense', and they need active preparation through simulation. This method can provide an opportunity to practise skills in a safe environment where students can make errors, without the danger of harm to themselves or their clients. This method can help them learn safely about how to deal with the unusual.

- *Teachable moments*
  Simulated learning offers the advantage of providing a quick response to the 'teachable moment', when students are especially receptive to a particular piece of learning. Perhaps an experience has allowed the student to recognise an issue that was not evident before. The student's learning can then be further developed in a concrete form by using a piece of simulated learning. In this way the practice teacher can exactly match the learning needs of a student with a learning opportunity. Simulated learning materials are very flexible because they can be used precisely when required.

- *Difficult areas of practice*
  There are some aspects of practice that are innately difficult to learn because of their intrinsic nature, such as professional values. Sometimes students may be expected to absorb the values of professional practice through working in the placement agency or through abstract discussion around codes of professional practice (BASW, 1986 (revised edition); IFSW, 1988; NASW, 1990). Learning about these difficult areas may be easier for students if they are presented as simulation exercises.

Using simulations – an example
There are very many different types of simulations, they may be: written exercises, pre-recorded trigger videos, role rehearsals for particular practice scenarios, in fact any medium may be used that is capable of providing students

with a representation of reality. The representation may highlight some feature of reality to provide an opportunity for students to focus on particular elements of practice.

A good simulation does not have to be a perfect replica of reality – quite the reverse, some of the most powerful simulations deliberately distort reality to promote learning. Also simulations may be used by social work students individually or in groups, with or without the practice teacher present. An example of a simulated piece of learning is presented below. This example is designed to help students grapple with some of the difficult problems that are associated with professional values and ethics. It uses the experience of eating – a universal human experience to pose questions about cultural differences.

You are what you eat

Explanation

You Are What You Eat stimulates students to think about their own cultural inheritance by focusing on the cultural significance of childhood meals. This is a trigger to think in broader terms of the impact of culture and the development of a 'cultural inventory' to help communities get in touch with their own unique cultural inheritance.

The Activity can have a powerful effect, so plenty of time and space should be allowed for students to express their thoughts and feelings.

Purpose

This activity is designed to sensitise students to cultural differences by understanding more about their own cultural inheritance. The student learns that cultural competence is not an absolute quality and that 'culture' is not something which is limited to certain groups, classes or 'races'.

Method

1. This activity is most effective if it can be done by a small group of students and practice teachers from diverse backgrounds. In this way, influences which individuals may well take for granted are put in perspective. It is a good exercise for pairs of practice teachers and students to do together early in the placement.
2. Give YOU ARE WHAT YOU EAT to the students and practice teachers with no prior preparation, other than a brief explanation of the purpose of the activity. Participants can work in pairs, threes or fours, but no larger.
3. Get feedback from everybody. Help the group to move out from the focus on meals towards broader considerations of the impact of culture as an active force in their lives. Encourage people to share any new understandings they have gained about themselves and other people. (Allow 45–60 minutes).

Variations

The experience of meals is universal and feels relevant to all individuals: a colloquium on food at Johns Hopkins University, Baltimore, in 1991 concluded that 'feeding and eating is really one with the human heart.'

In addition, experiences of music provide another opportunity to expose cultural influences. Early experiences of medicine (what was considered to be healthy or unhealthy, what were the family's pet cures?) are also enlightening.

The simulation

To prepare for this activity, put these meals in order for a typical day and add any meals which are not named: (for example, some South Walesians eat *tea-tea*, a meal of cold, sweet foods taken in the late afternoon):

* DINNER * BRUNCH * TEA * BREAKFAST * LUNCH *
ELEVENSES * SUPPER *

- As a child, which of these meals did you eat?
- What image does the word to describe each meal bring to mind?
- We only need to eat two meals a day, so why so many possible meals?
- Were there any periods of fast in your family?
- What was the main meal of the day in your family; who was present?
- On weekdays, was your main meal of the day at school or at home?
- Was there any special day of the week with different meal patterns?

Smells
- What are your earliest memories of food smells?
- What, if any, smells greeted you as you came home from school?
  are there any smells which have special memories for you?

Tastes
- What was your favourite-tasting food; was it associated with a family meal?
- Did your family encourage you to try unfamiliar foods and tastes?
- If you didn't like the taste of something on your plate, what happened?

Touch
- Did you have to wash your hands before coming to the table?
- What foods could you eat by hand at the main family meal?

- Were you ever hit for misbehaviour at the table? if so, what had you done?

Sounds
- Did your family make any blessing before eating?
- Were family meals times for conversation or silence?
- If conversational, were these happy, argumentative or a mix?

Sights
- Who prepared the meal, set the table and served the food?
- How was the table set – did you have a tablecloth, napkins, etc.?
- Would you often or seldom see guests eating with you at the family table?

How have the habits of your childhood meals influenced your adult meals? If you share meal-times with a partner, what similarities and differences did you notice in your meal-time behaviours? Have other cultures influenced the way you take the main meal of the day now, or is it very similar to your childhood experience?

This exercise is reproduced from Doel and Shardlow (1993).

Through using a simulation exercise such as this, students can learn much about their own cultural heritage. Without a sense of one's own culture, it is near impossible to recognise the influence and importance of culture to others. Developing this awareness helps students to develop the ability to work with clients in a culturally sensitive way. *You Are What You Eat* could be a useful introduction with students to move on from culturally sensitive practice to issues of power and oppression, especially the role of 'significant definers' in society. *You Are What You Eat* is especially revealing in terms of social class.

Simulations do not need to need to be elaborate. They

can be developed by individual practice teachers and students. For example, a practice teacher may keep some brief scenarios drawn from actual examples of social work practice to illustrate practice dilemmas. Students would respond to the problems presented in the scenarios, and the responses form a basis for discussion in a future practice tutorial. Developing a bank of simulations may be something that practice teachers complete over a number of placements, and students can, themselves, help to develop learning materials for future students on placement. There are parallels, too, with the methods of learning which practitioners undertake in order to become practice teachers (Doel and Shardlow, 1996).

Learning from published sources
An important source of learning for students is through the use of published materials of various types. Books, pre-recorded video or audio tape, photographs, legal documents, agency requirements and publicity or whatever, all have a useful part to play in a students' learning. They can provide a student with access to material that is not available in any other way, such as clients' accounts of their experiences or examples of good interviewing practice. The material does not have to be restricted to factual data: novels, poetry, plays and any of the arts can be useful in helping students to learn. These kinds of material can be used as background information, or as primary material to capture the essence of certain situations, when the professional literature is unavailable or requires supplementing. A particularly rich opportunity for using visual arts has been through group work with adolescents, where the use of cartooning, drama and creative writing has been substantial. There may have been some reluctance by practice teachers to make full use of written materials, either through lack of easy access to adequate library resources or because of beliefs that such materials are best approached in the college-based part of the curriculum. It is clear that the use of these kinds of material in agency settings is just as relevant.

Using different methods

Part of the fun of learning and teaching is to experiment with different methods of promoting learning, and there are many opportunities on placement. The *structured learning model* encourages practice teachers and students to experiment with different approaches of learning. A range of different methods can be used to meet the learning required by a practice curriculum.

The selection of methods need not be random, but can be in accord with the principles of *Harmony, Effectiveness, Efficiency* and *Linkage to the Curriculum.* In addition, there should be a balance between the different methods of learning, *Modelling, Enactment, Simulation,* and *Published Sources.* Relying too heavily on a particular method impoverishes the learning on placement. It is the challenge of all those involved in practice learning to find this balance to meet the learning needs of each student.

7

Examining Practice Competence

Summary

Examining the practice competence of social work students presents the practice teacher and student with a bewildering array of conceptual conundrums about the nature of social work, major moral questions about the ethics of assessment, and a morass of more mundane, if very practical, difficulties. In this chapter an attempt is made to grapple with these difficulties, by suggesting some practical principles to guide the selection of evidence and describing some of the possible methods of examining students' practice competence.

Examining practice competence

Practice teachers and students face a substantial range of difficulties in identifying evidence to indicate a student's level of practice competence. Some of these are technological problems, such as how to conduct a particular method of gathering evidence. For example, if a student is required to produce a video of their work and analyse it, they need to have an understanding of how to operate the video recorder and to have some guidelines for the analysis. However, there are deeper fundamental questions that bedevil the making of judgements about a student's competence, questions such as 'can we even agree about the nature of good social work practice?' and questions about the existence of different approaches to the measurement of competence, as exemplified at one extreme by the competency model, where small and discrete aspects of practice are measured, and at the other by holistic measurement of a range of skills and abilities. There are debates about new forms of measurement where the student is responsible for supplying the evidence rather than the practice teacher for collecting it. It is difficult to know where to break into some of these issues, so we begin by examining some of the conceptual problems surrounding the measurement of students' competence before considering some of the mechanisms and methods of measurement.

A first problem to resolve is the possibility of confusion resulting from the variety of terms used to describe the events and processes which comprise the measurement of practice competence. This is not just a source of irritation to practice teacher and student alike; it does have potentially serious consequences as real differences of meaning make for difficulties in securing a common understanding about the very nature, purpose and processes of the measurement of competence. As Brandon and Davies (1979) reported in their seminal study, no shared agreement among social work tutors, students and practice teachers existed about the fundamentals of the measurement of practice competence. Some interpreted assessment as:

> an *ongoing process* [original italics], with educational objectives in which the student's work and development are reviewed, his competence fostered, his weakness minimised, his knowledge increased. (Brandon and Davies, 1979, p. 296)

Alternatively, some thought that assessment was:

> an *event* [original italics], 'a system of testing and grading' which involves a judgement and a decision, which is an examination decision because student social workers must pass in their field practice as well as in theoretical studies. (p. 297)

An important conceptual distinction is evident in these two views. One sees assessment as part of an educational process which exists for the benefit of the learner, the other sees is as a judgement event, made at a given point in time, that specifies the level of attainment achieved by a student. The importance of this distinction is located in its consequences. As Syson and Baginsky (1981) found in their study of eight courses, some tutors failed to make adequate distinctions between their responsibilities to students to help educate them and responsibilities to the public to ensure that only the competent are allowed to practise, with the consequence that they were reluctant to fail students, almost in any circumstances. If the purpose of assessment is for the benefit of the learner, to enable further development, then there may be a reluctance to fail students. Alternatively, if judgements are made about actual levels of competence attained, and a required minimum standard exists, then the measurement of competence becomes a means to protect the public from incompetence and to validate those who have attained this level of competence.

There are then two discrete meanings of 'assessment'. In addition, Butler and Elliot regard assessment as having two key functions, 'evaluation' and 'examination'. Evaluation is a 'continuing process by which the student receives feedback' (Butler and Elliot, 1985, p. 75), whilst examination is an event that serves to protect the client. Ford and Jones (1987) agree that evaluation is to be understood as feedback to the student, but they regard assessment as the standard to be reached at the end of a placement or course. Pettes takes yet another different view, using evaluation and assessment interchangeably and suggesting that there are two purposes to evaluation:

> to judge the student's work and progress and to ensure that his [*sic*] educational needs are being met. (Pettes, 1979)

In these confused circumstances, there is no alternative but to define the terminology used in this book:

- *Examination* will be used to refer to the event at the end of a placement or course, when a judgement is reached about the level of professional competence attained by the student. The purpose of this event is to ensure that the public are protected from the incompetent practitioner. Thus, the examination of practice competence at the end of the course serves to exclude those from practice who have not attained the required standard and, of equal importance, it validates the competence of those who are successful. Using the word 'examination' does not imply anything about the way in which evidence of professional competence is best obtained; for example, it does not imply that there should be a traditional form of unseen written examination paper.
- *Appraisal* will be used to describe the process that should be continuous throughout the placement, whereby the practice teacher keeps the student informed of the quality of work done by the student. The intention in appraising performance is to tell the student how far the work being done is satisfactory, and to what extent the goals of the placement are being reached. The purpose of appraisal is to maximise the student's learning and to ensure that the student is clearly aware of what has been learned so that further knowledge, skills and values can be developed.
- *Assessment* will be used as a general term to encompass both examination and appraisal – its usage will be restricted.

Appraisal and examination are of equal importance, but they serve different functions. A student cannot learn without regular feedback through appraisal, nor can the public be protected without adequate structures and standards for examination. Some of the difficulties confronting the practice teacher in both appraising students' performance and examining practice competence are similar; for example, the complexities of obtaining samples of practice as evidence of the level of practice competence are common to both appraisal and examination. Equally, some aspects of appraisal and examination differ; for example, the 'rules' governing appraisal will differ considerably from those for conducting examinations.

Other major difficulties about the examination of practice competence have been identified:

- Little consensus exists among practitioners and academics about the nature of social work. The comment of David Millard's is as relevant now as when it as written:

  > Unfortunately, there is at present no satisfactory anatomy of professional competence such as might allow the measurement individually of its component parts. (1972, p. 13)

Millard's view is widely supported (Hayward, 1979; Syson and Baginsky, 1981; Goodall and Lenn, 1984; England, 1986; Kerr, 1988), nor is there any indication that we are any nearer to the goal of a universally accepted form of social work practice. It is difficult to share the optimism of Minty *et al.* (1988), who argued that such difficulties are exaggerated and reducible to disagreements over priorities. On the contrary, the complexity of social work seems to increase

- There is no agreement as to what constitutes competence in a novice social worker. This follows from the lack of agreement over the nature of social work practice itself. Without such an agreement it is difficult to develop criteria which accurately define the level of competence to be attained (Syson and Baginsky, 1981; Danbury, 1986; Minty, *et al.*, 1988). In the UK there has been an attempt by CCETSW (1991b) to define the basic level of competence
- The difficulties in obtaining reliable evidence about a student's competence are substantial. In their study of 35 marginal pass/fail students Brandon and Davies (1979) found it was often assumed that students should pass their course if no evidence of incompetence was presented. Whilst this notion may be consistent with

the principles of natural justice (that the accused are innocent until proved guilty), it is not an adequate basis on which to conduct the examination of practice competence in social work. Brandon and Davies advanced the argument that students could only be passed as competent if they produced *positive* evidence of competence; in other words, the presumption is that the student is not competent until proved otherwise. This principle has gradually gained acceptance and been incorporated into the majority of social work courses. However, despite this elegant principle, it may be asked 'what exactly is the evidence that a student needs to present, and how is it to be obtained?'

- The subjectivity of assessment: different practice teachers may form differing views about the quality of work done based upon similar pieces of evidence. There may be disturbingly wide variations in the grade awarded (Shardlow, 1989b). This variation between the judgements made by practice teachers is especially worrying, because often the practice teacher is the sole examiner of the student's practice competence.

We must now consider how far it is possible for the practice teacher and student to develop a working accommodation with these difficulties and to be able to examine practice competence in a way that promotes learning, yet ensures that adequate standards are maintained.

Triangulation – the examination of practice

The structured learning model incorporates three principles to guide the examination of practice competence. These are designed to help practice teachers and students make decisions about the level of competence demonstrated by individual students. Taken together, these three principles help to meet the criteria for good examination practice (Doel and Shardlow, 1989) and provide a way to clarify existing approaches to the examination.

The principles are as follows.

Principle one: the selection principle

> The nature of the skill, knowledge in practice or value to be examined is the major factor in determining the selection of the method of examination of practice competence.

To explain this principle, consider the following musical analogy:

- To examine a pianist's competence at playing the piano, it is essential to hear the pianist play; listening to pianists' self-reports of how they played would not provide evidence of the way they actually performed, but only of how they thought they had played. There may be a large gap between the pianist's self-perceptions and the views of the audience. Similarly, a written test would not measure a pianist's ability to play and interpret a piece of music, but would test the grasp of musical theory.

The same is true in regard to examining social work practice. In order to measure effectively and reliably whether a student is able to 'do' social work, a method of examining which provides direct access to the skill, knowledge in practice or value is needed – just as in the musical analogy.

The application of the selection principle to the examination of competence on placement would suggest that practice teachers and students ought to consider using methods of examination that provide direct access to the knowledge, skills and values that are being measured. However, evidence suggests that practice teachers have tended to show a preference for one form of examination, student self-report – usually presented to the practice teacher in practice tutorials.

Self-report by students often takes the form of verbal presentation, but this method of examination also includes students' written descriptions of work. Morell's study of 76 student placements found that 90 per cent of practice teachers were satisfied with student self-report (written or verbal) as the most important indicator of practice competence (1980). This finding was echoed by Akhurst, who reported heavy reliance on retrospective accounts by students as evidence of professional competence (1978). Similar results were found by Goodall and Lenn, whilst testing a task-based approach to the examination of students' practice competence:

> there is no doubt that we are still relying on the accuracy and integrity of students' own reports about their work. (1984, p. 220)

These findings demonstrated a consistent picture of practice teachers' heavy reliance, and in some cases dependence, upon retrospective student self-report as a method of examining competence. The arguments against this form of assessment have been presented elsewhere: in analogy (Doel, 1987b), in parody (Shardlow, 1989a) and more seriously (Shardlow and Doel, 1991). At the extreme, this method may be highly unreliable as Baird (1991) reports one instance of a student fabricating accounts of interviews that never took place. More routinely, this method may not really represent the real abilities of students, since students may be unduly self-critical in their self-reports. Evans (1987) reports a very much better performance by a student when directly observed in work with a client than predicted by the practice teacher, based upon student self-report and discussion in practice tutorials.

There is further indication of a mismatch between the quality of practice reported by students and that suggested by other methods of gathering evidence. One early study identified that even when students were attempting accurate recall through process recordings, a comparison with audio-tape of the same interview demonstrated that students omitted significant elements of the interview in their records (Wilkie, 1963). However, attempts have been made to argue for student self-report, albeit in a much refined form, through the viva voce, (Millard, 1972, 1978; Badger, 1991). It is desirable to encourage the development of self-monitoring as an attribute of a professional practitioner (Sheldon

and Baird, 1978). However, can this only be an acceptable method of examination when it is used in conjunction with other methods?

Since many of those studies were completed, several
changes have occurred. In particular, there is a national
requirement in the UK that a student's practice is 'directly and systematically' observed by a practice teacher
and that the evidence from these observations must be
included in the final report (CCETSW, 1991b, 1989). A
second major change has been the introduction of a national system of training for practice teachers (CCETSW,
1991a). There is as yet little evidence to indicate how
practice teachers' behaviour in judging students' competence has been affected. We do not know to what extent
different methods of examining students' competence are
being used or whether student self-report remains the
dominant method. However, practice teachers and
students might carefully consider the methods of examination to be used and relate these to the type of skill,
knowledge in practice or value to be examined. This would
limit the emphasis on approaches such as student self-
report as a method of examining practice skills, knowledge and values.

Principle two: the correspondence principle

> Correspondences between different pieces of evidence will
> indicate the actual level of student competence.

A major problem in the structure for examining students'
practice competence is the great reliance placed upon
the opinion of a single practice teacher. One response to
this difficulty has been the introduction of practice panels
to ensure that sufficient evidence has been presented by
a practice teacher to justify the recommendation made
about a student's competence; these panels serve to moderate standards across practice learning (Shardlow, 1987;
Borland *et al.*, 1988; Minty *et al.*, 1988). However, such
solutions are remedial rather than addressing the problem at source; these panels tend to scrutinise evidence

provided by practice teachers and do not have direct access to students' practice except through the evidence presented by practice teachers. This does not seem to be fair on the student.

To begin to resolve this problem, it is useful to reconceptualise the activity of the practice teacher. Instead of assuming that the practice teacher's function is to report the student's level of competence with supporting evidence, it is possible to imagine the practice teacher and student jointly engaged in a piece of research to identify the student's level of practice competence. The correspondence principle guides the search for evidence, so practice teachers and students can seek to identify correspondences between different pieces of evidence about competence. This helps to provide firm indications of the level of competence possessed by a student.

Let us look at an example to illustrate this point:

- A practice teacher and student wish to identify evidence that the student is able to communicate effectively with clients. A variety of examination methods may be used, including: listening to what the student reports about such interactions; receiving formal written opinions from colleagues who have direct access to the student's practice; observing the student's practice and interviewing clients. (Few accounts exist of the structured use of clients' opinions to measure students' competence. Furniss (1988) offers practice guidance and has described its use in probation, whilst Baird (1991) reports a research study of 227 clients of 34 students who were interviewed.)

In this example, the practice teacher and student must choose the *method* of measuring competence (for example, direct observation, audio-tape, structured exercise – Catherine Sawdon (1985) has termed these 'action techniques'), and the *source* of evidence (student, practice teacher, client, carer, colleague). If there is a correspondence in the nature of evidence obtained from at least two different sources, ideally using different examination methods, practice teacher and student can be reasonably confident that the level of the student's practice competence has been correctly identified. Where there is a disagreement between the evidence from different sources, the practice teacher and student have an indication that closer investigation is required and more evidence must be sought using other examples of the student's practice.

Of course, it will not be possible to obtain evidence for all areas of competence in such a comprehensive fashion, so the practice teacher and student must carefully select how the student's practice is to be sampled over the placement, that is, the selection of representative examples of practice. In making this selection the practice teacher needs to apply the selection principle: the nature of the skill, knowledge in practice, or value to be examined is the paramount factor in the selection of the method of examination of practice competence.

A working hypothesis suggests that the larger the number of sources of evidence which correspond with each other, the more likely it is that the level of practice competence has been correctly identified.

This process of collecting opinions from different sources of evidence and using different methods in a systematic way gives rise to the term '**examination by triangulation**'. 'Triangulation' is derived from processes of mapping unknown territory in land surveys (the same term is also used to describe modes of research that derive information from several different sources – where each one forms a check on the others).

Measurements can be taken from different points to map the territory by identifying the position of key landmarks. A minimum of three measurements from two fixed points is needed to determine the position of any third point in a geographical survey (the distance between the fixed points must be measured as must the distance from each fixed point to the unknown point). Similar principles apply in the measurement of students' practice competence, though it is much easier to measure land than student competence! Land is a fixed physical entity, student competence is more abstract and subjective. Hence, when seeking to fix the point of student competence, a minimum of two measurements from different positions (using different methods as well as knowing the 'distance' between the two methods) is necessary to determine competence for any particular skill area, aspect of knowledge or value dimension. Only then can a satisfactory level of reliability be ensured, especially if one of the measures used is student self-report. However, practice teachers and students will have to reconcile the demands of an ideal system with what is practically possible on placement.

Only a relatively small number of skill areas, aspects of knowledge or values can be measured using the correspondence principle, because of the limited time available for examination on placement. To apply the correspondence principle, it is useful to focus on a few skills, values or aspects of knowledge. The trick is to select the *core indicators for examination*, that is, those skills, aspects of knowledge or values that are fundamental to social work practice. For example, the ability to structure an intervention with a client might be a core indicator because it is inconceivable that a competent social worker should not possess this ability. Likewise, in selecting which elements to examine, practice teachers can greatly simplify the examination task by seeking 'examination overlap', where the testing of aspects of competence effectively measures several dimensions of practice ability.

Principle three: the sampling principle

> Examination events should be distributed throughout a placement on an agreed schedule to sample practice effectively.

Sampling a student's work should be undertaken throughout the placement. For many aspects of practice a student can be expected to demonstrate competence on one, two or at most three occasions. The practice teacher will then have sufficient evidence of competence (if the correspondence principle is employed). However, there are some dimensions of practice that need to be demonstrated throughout *all* aspects of practice. For example, the student must always demonstrate the ability to work in a way that shows awareness of the existence of socially structured difference.

On a placement, the practice teacher should take, or a student provide, *measured samples* of practice at specific points in time during the placement. A measured sample is the collection of a piece of evidence about a student's competence in performing a particular skill, using a piece of knowledge or demonstrating a grasp of professional values. For example, a measured sample might be the direct observation by the practice teacher of a student's interview with a client, where the focus of the observation is to examine the student's ability to review achievements jointly with the client. Students need to be informed at the start of the placement about the content and nature of the examination events; only then can they adequately prepare for these examinations. Also, they need to know when their practice will be sampled during the placement, and have the opportunity to influence these decisions; through such mechanisms it is possible to promote fairness in the examination of practice competence.

The practice teacher and student together can agree a programme for the taking of measured samples throughout the placement. Students should not be overburdened with examination tasks, so there must be sufficient opportunity to learn without the worry of constant examination. Similarly, there is a logic to the timing of taking measured samples – some skills, knowledge in practice or values can most conveniently be measured at an early point in the placement; others – perhaps the more complex aspects of practice – towards the end. In whatever way the practice teacher and student agree to distribute the collection of evidence, it should be an open process, agreed by both parties. Based upon their past experience, practice teachers will usually offer proposals about the arrangements for examination. However, it is important that students' views are also taken into account, if the method and processes of examination are to be seen as legitimate by all parties.

Triangulation in action: a brief example

Let us consider a relatively simple example of examination by triangulation as it might be implemented. Suppose a practice curriculum includes a requirement to enable the student to learn about a method of social work practice. In this example, the practice teacher's preferred method of work is task-centred practice and this is routinely offered to students. The practice teacher informs the student that there will be an examination of the student's ability to plan work with clients over time using this method (Doel and Marsh, 1992). Practice teacher and student then jointly agree when and how this examination is to occur.

The practice teacher suggests that this skill will be examined about a third of the way into the placement and the student agrees. After the student has been on placement a few weeks, and has been observed in practice (to accustom the student to this process), the practice teacher and student decide how to conduct the examination of skills in exploring problems (one part of the task-centred method). They agree that student self-report is inadequate as a sole indicator, because this would not validate the student's competence. As part of this process, the practice teacher explains the essence of examination by triangulation and together they review possibilities to gain evidence: for example, live observation by the practice teacher, audio-tape, video-tape, observation by colleagues, student self-report and analysis.

Given that the skill to be measured is an interactional one with clients, they agree that the student's performance must be observed and decide, using principle one (the selection principle), to identify the range of methods that could be used. They agree that video-tape would be ideal, but impractical in this particular case, so they consider other possible ways of observing the student's practice. To take account of principle two (the correspondence principle), they establish a range of different sources of evidence and decide that the practice teacher will observe an interview by 'sitting in', and that a different session will be audio-taped. The practice teacher agrees to write a brief analysis of the student's work in the chosen skill area, and this is to be incorporated directly into the final report.

A colleague, having first been fully prepared, is asked to listen to the first fifteen minutes of the audio-tape and to write a brief commentary, which is also to be included in the final report. The student is asked to compare performance in the two interviews, very briefly in writing. They agree the timing of these measured samples of practice well in advance of the actual dates, to ensure that principle three (the sampling principle) is followed. The collection of evidence for this skill is co-ordinated with the planned collection of other *measured samples* of other skills, knowledge in practice or professional values during the placement – thus ensuring that the student is not overburdened by having to provide too much evidence of competence in different aspects of practice all at the same time.

When the practice teacher has all the material from the three points of view, correspondences – or their lack – will be identified, according to the correspondence principle. There is no need for the practice teacher to listen to the audio-tape, unless there is doubt about the student's competence.

This example has illustrated one way in which the triangulation can be arranged in quite an elaborate way. Other simpler approaches are also possible; for example, all three participants could have independently formed their own opinion based on the same material – in this case, the audio-tape of the same interview. From these three pieces of evidence the practice teacher would then seek out the correspondences. Where a correspondence is found between different pieces of evidence, the practice teacher and student can be reasonably confident that the student's practice competence in that skill, aspect of knowledge or value dimension has been correctly identified. Where no such correspondence exists and the pieces of evidence are incompatible with each other, further investigations must be made. Perhaps there is genuine disagreement about the student's level of competence; for example, a colleague and a client may have very different views about what constitutes good practice and this may be reflected in the evidence they present about the student. Perhaps the student's performance may actually vary in performing the same skill, demonstrating a professional value or using a piece of practice knowledge from one occasion to another for a number of reasons: some work is more difficult than others; performing new tasks to high levels of competence is implicitly difficult; or the student may have personal problems that influence practice. In either case, the practice teacher must weigh the evidence carefully, and it may then be necessary to seek further evidence from another source.

The triangulation offers the potential for a creative approach to the examination of students' practice competence. We will now examine some of the different methods of examination that are available.

Methods of examination

There are several different methods of examining the practice competence of social work students that can be used in conjunction with the three examination principles. Whatever method is used it is essential to ensure that any judgements made are grounded on firm evidence. There are many ways to categorise the various methods of examination; Evans (1991) lists the following:

- assignments
- direct access to students practice
- oral presentation
- practice outcome
- client feedback
- student self-assessment
- peer assessment
- portfolios

Whatever categorisation is adopted there are a large

number of different methods of examining students' practice competence. Rather than generate an exhaustive list we have grouped the various methods not tidily, but out of convenience. Nevertheless, it provides the opportunity to explore the application of a range of different methods of examination to social work practice. These are now examined in turn.

Practice outcome

The first group of methods are those that measure the outcome or effect of a particular piece of practice. The outcome of a piece of social work practice may be measured in different ways. Two of the most important are: the use of objective indicators, such as in probation practice, where clients' recidivism rates are taken as a measure of effectiveness in reducing crime (such measures may be controversial); subjectively, by recording in some way clients' opinions about the quality of service received. Various parties might have a legitimate claim to advance views about the key indicators of a satisfactory outcome. Here the discussion will be limited to clients' views regarding practice outcome – largely because despite the current rhetoric enshrined in words such as 'partnership with clients' or the 'empowerment of clients', too little attention is given to involving clients in the process of examining students' practice competence.

There is a dearth of any published material reporting examples of practice teachers who have successfully incorporated clients' opinions in the examination of practice competence. Recent texts on practice learning (Butler and Elliot, 1985; Danbury, 1986; Ford and Jones, 1987) are silent on this topic, omitting to mention the role of clients in assessment altogether (Shardlow and Doel, 1992a). Where clients are currently involved in the examination of practice competence, it is generally in an unstructured and *ad hoc* manner. Final placement reports about students sometimes include a brief comment from a client about the student. Most usually, these comments will have been obtained by the practice teacher through a range of unplanned actions, such as a chance encounter with the client, a letter of complaint or praise, or perhaps a hurried remark at the end of a joint interview with the student. Chance opinion, gathered in this fashion, is unlikely to indicate anything of reliable significance about practice competence, unless it is a report of sheer bad practice.

Such chance comments usually provide an unrepresentative sample of all the clients the student will have worked with on a placement. Moreover, the comments are unlikely to cover more than a small aspect of the student's practice and it is unethical to use such chance comments as the basis for judgements about practice competence, because to do so would be unjust to the student. Comments of this nature cannot be taken to represent a true spread of the student's practice skills, values or knowledge with a sufficiently broad range of clients. They may be useful only as 'pointers' that require further elaboration.

What kind of results might be expected from incorporating clients' opinions about the outcome of social work? One research study of 227 clients demonstrated that more than half of the clients were either completely or virtually satisfied. In contrast, only twelve clients had serious complaints (Baird, 1991, p. 32). This level of satisfaction is reassuring, but this research does not help the practice teacher and student methodologically to look at clients' views of practice outcome on placement.

How might the practice teacher seek the opinions of clients in a more formalised way rather than relying on chance events? One practice teacher, Furniss (1988), working in probation practice, has developed a structured approach to involving clients in the examination of student's practice competence. Towards the end of a placement, she interviews two clients of each student placed in her unit, one that she chooses and one chosen by the student. She admits that two is not really sufficient, but time constraints make it difficult to manage more. The student first seeks the client's agreement to participate and then the client receives a formal invitation by letter from the practice teacher to attend the office. The practice teacher seeks information about the following areas in an unstructured interview:

Furniss's method for obtaining clients' opinions of students' competence

1. I begin by explaining who I am and the purpose of the interview. I indicate that I am seeking the views of several people and I reassure them that their comments alone will not result in the student failing the placement, but will be helpful in indicating how the student may do the job better. I then wait for a response before continuing;

2. I seek their comments about their perceptions of Probation Orders, either from their own experience or their imagination before they meet the student, and ask how the reality differs or is the same, etc.;

3. I ask if the student explained the Probation Order to them at the beginning, particularly if the student prepared the SER.[1] I ask did they understand the student's explanation and has the reality been pretty much as they described it? What had been the surprises, the differences etc., etc.?

4. I ask them if a friend of theirs was placed on probation and said that the student was to be their Probation Officer and asked what they were like, what would the client say, how would they describe the student? I pursue that seeking clarification and asking them for examples or illustrations of their comments;

5. I ask them to say something they really like that the student does well and something that they ought to change or which they could improve;

---

1. SER: an abbreviation for social enquiry report, now replaced by the presentence report (PSR) – reports prepared to advise the courts how to sentence a person brought before the court.

6. I ask them that looking back over the period they have been on probation has it been helpful and in what kind of ways.

(Furniss, 1988, p. 2)

This approach could be developed further so that more of the questions might relate to outcome, rather than to the process of work done; or the interview might take a more structured form. To use this approach in a different setting it would be necessary to modify the questions. It would be a useful exercise for practice teacher and student together to develop the questions to be asked, as part of an 'outcome interview'. When conducting these interviews it is possible to think of the practice teacher being a 'researcher' of a student's practice competence, drawing on the literature available about research interviews.

Whatever the limitations of the approach, as outlined by Furniss, it is a step in the right direction. For, as she comments, none of the clients asked have refused to be interviewed. Most express surprise and pleasure at the request to offer opinions about students' competence. This type of assessment is in its infancy, but the signs are encouraging that it provides an important approach to the examination of practice competence. It is only one method of using outcome as an indicator of student competence.

Student self-report

Despite the comments earlier in the chapter, student self-report represents an important source of evidence, provided it is not over-used.

The most usual type of student self-report occurs when students give a report on their work as a part of the practice tutorial. There are many difficulties with student self-appraisal as a method of examination, for example:

● recall of a past interaction by a participant is imperfect and patchy; any self-analysis based upon recall will be flawed to some extent

- the astute student will usually be aware of the elements of good practice that the practice teacher expects to see, so these are likely to be highlighted by the student, and the less satisfactory elements ignored in the account given (this is true regardless of whether the report is verbal or written). Students find themselves having to satisfy practice teachers who are both enablers and examiners; in these circumstances, it is not surprising that students will seek to provide practice teachers with material that will meet the practice teachers' expectations
- there are indications that judgements made by practice teachers may be unreliable when compared with evidence drawn from direct observation; also, that judgements made by practice teachers, on the basis of student self-report, may underestimate students' abilities (Evans, 1987)

Despite these difficulties, it is possible to make positive use of student self-report as one dimension of examination. If there is proper planning to prepare for the self-report it may prove to be useful.

Consider the following example to illustrate how self-report can provide evidence of competency:

- A practice teacher and student agree that the student will undertake a particular task with a client. They also agree the aspects of practice that the student will report on, and the method of self-report, whether verbal or written. In addition they agree the criteria of good practice for measuring the skills, knowledge or values to be examined, so that the student has a clear understanding about the qualities to report on. Thus both student and practice teacher have a shared understanding of the examination event. It has formal and planned qualities and does not consist of a casual, spontaneous self-report given to the practice teacher.

Observed performance

In the UK direct observation of a student social worker's practice with clients became a mandatory feature of the examination of practice competence only relatively recently (CCETSW, 1989). Hostility to the notion, often on ethical grounds, has previously restricted wide-scale use of this method. Evans (1991) suggests that the reluctance to use this method may not have entirely subsided. There is as yet only a limited, but growing, experience among practice teachers about how to examine in this way, and very little published material exists. Three different approaches to the direct observation of practice can be identified.

1. The fly on the wall
In this approach, the student is observed by a practice teacher who is in the same room as the student and the client. This approach has always been possible in group care, where practice takes place in a public arena. Its introduction to individual and family work is still more experimental. The presence of the practice teacher will affect the interaction of student and client to some degree, so a major task for the practice teacher is to minimise this, such that the encounter is as natural as practicable. The practice teacher may use different styles of observation, from sitting in a corner saying nothing, to making the occasional intervention. Where practice teachers intervene during the interaction, the quality of evidence about students' competence will be reduced. The fact that the method of examination influences the interaction between student and client does not invalidate the use of this method, since all methods of examination influence to some extent the performance of the student.

2. Collaborative work
When students and practice teachers jointly work on shared pieces of work there are ample opportunities for the students' practice to be observed. Good examples of this are where student and practice teacher together organise and facilitate a group, or where both are co-workers with

a family. A complication with this approach to direct observation is that there are difficulties in separating the
examination of practice from ongoing processes of learning, because it is often the case that the practice teacher
and student will work together over several sessions with
a client or groups of clients.

A further difficulty arises that where practice teacher
and student are working together, they are jointly providing a service to the client. This makes for more difficulty for practice teachers, because they have simultaneously
to observe and record the nature of the student's practice whilst being engaged themselves in providing a service directly to the client. A final problem is that, to some
extent, the practice teachers are also measuring their own
practice. This method needs to be handled with care.

3. Technologically assisted

A variety of different technologies exist to help the practice teacher observe a student, one-way screens, audio-
tape and video-tape being the most common. The one-way
screen attempts to resolve problems associated with the
practice teacher's presence in the same room, though
clients and students still know that they are being watched
or recorded, and this can have some impact on the situation. The use of audio- and video-tape can be helpful
methods of 'capturing' the student's performance, and
their importance lies in allowing live practice to be seen
and marked by two or more practice teachers, in much
the same fashion as for written assignments. Also, the
evidence of a student's competence is retained for further scrutiny, which is of particular importance where the
student's work is seen as being marginal.

Using direct observation

To use all direct observational methods successfully there
are some important principles to take account of:

- *Ethical concerns* These methods involve the client in
  an obvious way in the gathering of information about
  a student's practice competence. Sensitive information

may be collected about the client and stored on various magnetic media. Clients must give written permission for this to happen, and they need to be given clear information about a range of different issues, such as who will watch the material, the uses to which it will be put, and the final disposal of any recordings. Students also have rights! They should be treated in exactly the same manner and have formal agreements and full information about all of these issues. Similar concerns apply when conducting 'live observation in the same room'

- *Student stress*   Examinations are stressful for most people, and direct observation of performance is particularly difficult for the examinee! This stress can be minimised by familiarisation with the process of examination. If students' practice is only observed at the point of examination, students will be unused to that situation, and at some risk of not performing as well as might be expected. If practice is observed regularly, students will have the opportunity to become as comfortable as possible with the experience. Where direct observation relies upon the successful use of audio- or video-tape, students need the opportunity to practise with the equipment to attain an acceptable level of technological proficiency

- *Criteria for good practice*   In all examinations, students need to have very clear information both about how they will be graded and what will be the subject-matter of the examination. This presents problems in the examination of social work, since there is a wide divergence of opinion about what constitutes acceptable social work practice and some evidence that practice teachers grade the same sample of work differently (Shardlow, 1989b). We cannot be too sanguine about overcoming all of these difficulties.

However, if prior to the examination event, practice teacher and student have agreed the specific areas of competence to be examined and if they have jointly agreed the criteria to be used in evaluating the piece of practice, then the student will have a reasonable chance of demonstrating accurately his or her competence

- *Recording* Whichever approach to examining competence is selected, practice teacher and student need to be clear about how the results of the examination are to be recorded. This is less of a problem where audio- or video-tape is used, as a continuing record of the student's competence is created. However, where practice is directly observed in the same room the record of student competence may be dependent upon the quality and reliability of the practice teacher's memory. If possible, some type of grading schedule should be used and completed during the observation by the practice teacher. This may be difficult, but the effort is worthwhile.

These methods of observing a student's practice are important for validating professional competence. At present our knowledge of how best to integrate these methods is limited.

Written assignments

The examination of practice by written assignments may not seem a likely method to use, since it conjures images of national written examinations taken by people in their mid-teens, with a lasting horror of this form of examination. However, these skills relate directly to the requirements of being a social work practitioner, since a substantial part of social work requires the ability to produce various types of written work (such as recordings of work, reports for courts, internal committee reports, and possibly press releases). It is reasonable, therefore, that students demonstrate their competence in these areas. Other forms of assignment can also be used to simulate aspects of practice.

In reviewing this method of examination, Evans suggests three difficulties with written forms of examination:

- able practitioners may be penalised where their educational experience does not include an emphasis on writing
- undue emphasis on writing may have the effect of being

　　discriminatory against some groups on the grounds of
　　'race' or social class
● in the world of social work practice the spoken work
　is the preeminent form of communication (Evans, 1991,
　p. 45)

There is truth in these arguments, yet if the examination
of social workers' practice does not include written elements, students will not have the opportunity to demonstrate skills, knowledge and values which are *necessary* for
practice. We need to establish ways to diminish the possible disadvantages which Evans cites.

Peer review

The idea of examination by peers seems ideologically attractive, since it combines notions of fairness and partici-
pation. As the placement is less likely to be such an
individualised experience in the future (there are increasing
opportunities for several students to be placed with one
practice teacher), more opportunities are available for
students to review each other's practice. Evans (1991) suggests
that peer review has some advantages such as providing
increased responsibility for students and empowering students
to provide constructive comments to each other. When
asked retrospectively, students have indicated that they
thought that peers passed their professional qualification
when they ought not to have done (Davies, 1984b), which
is an implied criticism of the ability to examine competence.
　If peer assessment is to be used its value must depend
very heavily upon the quality of evidence available to
students, and there may be a danger that opinions about
professional competence could be shaped not so much
by evidence of performance with clients but according to
peer group politics. This is an area where more research
would be valuable, to illustrate how practice teachers and
students have used, and might use, peer review to provide evidence of practice competence.

Systematic examination

The structured learning model incorporates a systematic approach to assessment – both appraisal and examination. Careful selection of the methods and the sources of evidence is necessary, as is the application of the three principles of examination. The model also suggests the use of a balanced range of methods of examination throughout a placement. Besides a structured approach to examination, regular appraisal of the student is vital to maintain enthusiasm and to promote learning.

Developing systematic approaches to examination requires practice and effort on the part of students and practice teachers. Likewise, there must be an openness in the conduct of the examination of students' practice competence; this is challenging even in routine circumstances where failure is considered unlikely. When there is a possibility of failure, the associated emotions can become almost impossible to handle. We can all celebrate the success of a student who has provided evidence to be judged competent, but making the decision that someone is not competent evokes many different reactions. In these circumstances, practice teachers and students alike need to look to colleagues to ensure that procedures are adhered to and that the personal costs are not left for the individuals alone to deal with.

8

Difficulties with Learning: What Can Go Wrong?

Summary

This chapter examines some of the difficulties that confront students in their practice learning. There are very many reasons why learning on placement may be difficult. One of these, starting a placement and making the transition to learning on a placement, is discussed in some detail. Also, an approach is suggested to help students and practice teachers resolve difficulties with learning.

What can go wrong with learning?

Learning about social work practice on placement can be difficult and hard. At times students may doubt why they embarked on a career in social work, and practice teachers might wonder why they decided to teach, when they could have maintained a quiet life in practice with clients! If learning is not progressing well, action needs to be taken by practice teachers and students to maximise the opportunities provided by the placement. It is not possible to identify and list all the problems that might occur, so we have selected two as examples: the difficulties associated with starting a placement (an especially challenging time), and some of the barriers to learning that may be present or develop during a placement.

Starting to learn on placement

A new venture always presents challenges. The start of a placement is no exception and if it goes well it can set the climate for positive learning for the rest of the placement. Similarly, if the beginning goes badly, the rest of the placement can be adversely affected. For most students, beginning a period of practice learning in an agency will be a time for enthusiasm and excitement, but also one of stress and worry. Particular challenges confront all social work students as they start a placement. During the relatively short space of time encompassed within a placement a student is expected to:

1. grapple with a new area of work
2. make working relationships with a new group of colleagues
3. achieve a working familiarity with an unknown organisational structure, its policy, practices and procedures.

Students must engage with these learning tasks very quickly at the beginning of the placement, in the knowledge that at the end of the placement their level of competence in these areas will be examined. How many colleagues would like to be judged so comprehensively and so quickly?

Accounts by students of their experiences on placement do not usually provide much information about starting a placement. Research knowledge provides very general, retrospective accounts of the placement experience (Davies, 1984b), an analysis of specific aspects of the learning process, for example, the experience of different teaching methods (Rosenblatt and Meyer, 1975), or comparisons between learning in different types of placement, for example, comparing placements in student units with those provided by individual practice teachers (Richardson, 1982). However, in his study of 148 students, completing a social work course in 1980, Davies found that the majority thought that the placements were the most enjoyable part of the course, the most useful and indeed the best taught (Davies, 1984b, p. 16).

Although the placement is part of a more extensive course, it may be perceived as a relatively discrete element of learning by students, not least because it requires a fresh start with a new group of colleagues in a different physical environment and the completion of novel work tasks. Hence, the start of the placement may evoke similar feelings and responses in students to the outset of any new learning experience, such as the start of a course.

Rogers (1977), looking at experiences of students at the start of new courses through the writings (self-reports) of both students and teachers, found anxiety was a striking feature of adult learners. This was true across the spectrum of ability. The causes of this anxiety were fears of appearing stupid, a lack of confidence in discussing opinions, concern that peers will judge contributions to classes harshly or unfavourably, a fear of being a source of laughter, and expectations that written work would reveal superficiality or lack of ability.

One student is quoted by Rogers:

> For months before this training course I started to dream about looking stupid on it, and of making it look that I was incapable of doing the job. I was astonished at myself – a Cambridge first and all – being so worried about going 'back to school', but I used to think to myself, oh well, in another three months, two months, one month, it'll all be over. (1977, p. 33)

Neither teacher nor student can assume that adult learners, with high intelligence and proven academic abilities, will be exempt from such anxieties, nor does it follow that all students will experience anxiety. Rogers quotes a recent graduate who wrote about a new learning experience:

> I was really looking forward to joining the class and learning a new subject. I did not feel at all nervous as I have walked into many a lecture hall, and felt fully capable of tackling anything the lecturers was prepared to give me. (1977, p. 35)

Here, familiarity with the learning environment seems to have insulated the student from a sense of anxiety and indeed to have generated a perception of learning as a positive challenge. Some students, especially those from an identifiable minority, may experience the obverse of this, based on previous experience of being in learning environments which have not generated a sense of familiarity and comfort: for example, black students may have fears about the extent to which the curriculum will reflect their experience, or whether they will be subject to racism from colleagues or tutors, in the assessment processes or wherever. As Hamilton de Galle, a black social work student, wrote:

> Black students have been made to jump through more hoops than white students. Unreasonable amounts of work are placed on black students. Scrutiny of black students' personal activity is much tighter, while at the same time they are allowed to fall into bad practice and be disciplined or failed. (1991, p. 109)

All students will approach a new experience of learning with some expectations based upon their own past history of learning. As Cox writes:

> Students come to courses, not as *tabula rasa* waiting to have professional knowledge and skills imprinted upon them, but with specific educational biographies of their own and with ambiguous, problematic expectations. (1982, p. 394)

At the start of a placement, each student is likely to experience some of these feelings. There can be no standard response to the start of a placement, since this would presume that there is a stereotypical student. Practice teacher and student need to consider the individual student's prior learning experiences and orientation to learning. These considerations are not limited to the particular learning strategies preferred by the student (see Chapter 4) but should include the emotional and attitudinal responses to the process of being on placement. The practice teacher is a relative stranger, and it is not easy to discuss personal, perhaps painful, feelings in these circumstances. An example will illustrate this:

Jane, a 35 year old non-graduate social work student with a substantial career in sales and marketing, found the transformation to the role of student difficult to negotiate. Beginning a placement provided the opportunity to slough off the 'role of student' and to reassume the role of 'competent colleague'. Many who become social work students will have been working as practitioners within the personal social services, sometimes for many years, and the transition from competent practitioner and respected colleague to novice can be especially hard to accept. For some students, the skills of study will have decayed, others may never have become proficient at learning. How students approach new learning opportunities will vary greatly. Some may find learning easy, some difficult; for some it will present a challenge, for others an ordeal.

Practice teachers and students must work together to create a positive start to the placement. This can only be achieved if the student is recognised as having a personal history which encompasses established learning patterns, regular emotional responses to new situations, a wealth of previous experience, and the possession of a range of abilities. These characteristics may serve either to positively promote learning or may hinder progress. In either case, practice teachers can help the student to identify particular response patterns to learning. If these are positive they can be used to advantage, if negative they require resolution. In the next section some of the ways of resolving difficulties either at the start or later in placements are examined.

Learning difficulties identified

Sometimes a student does not progress during the placement, and there is little or no evidence of the student learning new skills or abilities. Ford and Jones (1987) identify eleven common difficulties that can adversely influence students' practice learning. These are: anxiety;

difficulty in producing written work; student fears about dealing with aggression; avoidance of supervision; very independent students; reliance on only one method; avoidance of involvement with clients; over-identification with clients; over-assertion; the influence of past experiences; and personal difficulties (Ford and Jones, 1987). This represents a very diverse collection of difficulties that students might face, some connected to the student's personality, others related to environmental influences, and others to the nature of the relationship between the practice teacher and student. It is difficult for a list of common learning problems to be comprehensive, because there are so many possible difficulties that a student might experience on placement. A way of understanding the difficulties in learning that a student might have on placement is required, and one which does not depend on providing a list of potential problems.

It can be difficult for both practice teacher and student to recognise when this situation is happening, since both parties are likely to have an emotional investment in the success of the placement, and so be reluctant to deal with the problems. If these difficulties are to be resolved, early identification and acknowledgement is desirable. The nature of students' and practice teachers' responses to difficulties in learning will, in large measure, be influenced by their beliefs about the causes of these difficulties and the possibility of effecting change. There are different theoretical approaches to help provide an understanding of these difficulties. One strand tends to locate difficulties in learning with the learner. An example of this approach can be found in the work of Megginson and Boydell, who identify four *blocks* to learning and suggest that:

> we all suffer to some extent from a number of blocks to learning that tend to prevent us from making full use of the various learning situations in which we find ourselves. (1989, p. 7)

Blocks to learning are not abnormal, but affect everybody; it is only the degree of difficulty experienced by each individual that varies. Megginson and Boydell describe four types of learning block:

Perceptual
Where learners cannot see or recognise the nature of learning required, or where inferences made following observations are inaccurate because of learners' expectations about what they expected to observe.

Cultural
When a learner rigidly adheres to a set of norms that define what is good or bad, these cultural norms may interfere with the learner's ability to acquire new skills.

Emotional
The emotional state of the learner affects the ability to learn; for example, if the learner is fearful of the consequences of failure, the ability to learn will be inhibited.

Intellectual
Here Megginson and Boydell do not just refer to the innate mental ability of the learner, although that will be a factor, but also to whether the learner has the intellectual skills required for a particular learning task, such as the mathematical skills to be able to learn a complex piece of geometry.

These definitions of different types of learning blocks offered by Megginson and Boydell seem plausible, and could be used by practice teachers and students to categorise difficulties experienced by students on placement. This type of formulation implies that the student possesses these blocks to learning (i.e. that they are the student's problem), so the student must be freed or released from the blocks to achieve learning. Moreover, it is the responsibility of the practice teacher to help the student overcome these difficulties. According to Megginson and Boydell there are different strategies to be used depending on the nature of the block identified.

Another approach to understanding difficulties with learning can be found in the work of Rowntree (1991), who suggests that students should identify for themselves *barriers* that have prevented learning. A *barrier* to learning is not just an attribute of the learner but may reside in any factor of the learner's world that inhibits learning: for example, it may be the way in which learning materials are presented. Rowntree suggests ten common barriers that students often confront:

- Lack of information about the availability of learning opportunities.
- Course content is unsuitable and does not provide the opportunity to learn the knowledge, skills or values that the learner wishes to acquire.
- Methods of learning used are unhelpful for learners.
- A gap between the qualifications of the learner and the qualifications needed for a particular course of study.
- The learning opportunities are not available at a suitable time.
- The geographical location of learning is not acceptable to the learner for whatever reason.
- The financial costs of learning are too great.
- The learner has anxieties about learning, perhaps based upon past experiences.
- Domestic circumstances may influence the ability to learn in a variety of ways.
- The learning environment may not be easy to negotiate if the learner has a physical disability.

These are not offered as a definitive list of all possible *barriers* to learning, but represent some of the common examples, drawn not specifically from practice learning but from the experience of all adult learners. This list of possible *barriers* to learning is broad, it encompasses a greater range of difficulties than the *blocks* to learning identified by Megginson and Boydell.

Rowntree's conceptualisation gives us a fuller understanding of the difficulties that students experience with their learning. However, rather than use the word *barrier* which has the ring of something that is firm and fixed, the term *obstacles* is preferred: that is, something that is

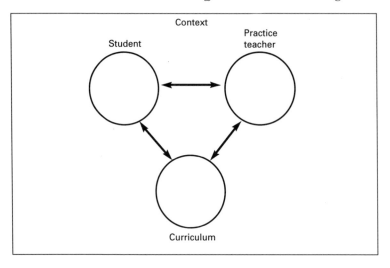

Figure 8.1 *The system of learning on placement*

in the way of learning but is capable of being removed, got round or over. There is no attempt to provide a comprehensive list of obstacles that students are likely to encounter in their practice learning, but practice teachers and students need strategies to help identify and overcome these obstacles to practice learning. Before developing these strategies it is helpful to consider some of the causes of obstacles to learning.

On placement, the student can be seen as at the centre of an interactive system of learning. If the student is to learn effectively, all parts of this system must function effectively and in harmony. There are four elements in the system: the student, the practice teacher, the curriculum and the context for learning. The four elements can be represented in the diagram shown in Figure 8.1.

Obstacles that prevent the student from learning may be present in any of the elements of the system that together create the total learning environment. Examples of possible obstacles in different parts of the system are:

Student

- Has worries about returning from the placement to collect children from a child minder and cannot concentrate at certain parts of the day
- Is over-anxious about the possibility of failure due to past experiences of learning.

Practice teacher

- Is always busy and gives the impression of having other things to do during the practice tutorial
- Does not give positive feedback but only negative comment when the student has not performed according to expectations.

Context

- The organisational environment of the placement is hostile to students
- The library does not contain enough relevant books.

Curriculum

- The way in which learning expectations are stated is unclear
- methods of learning are not diverse and do not fit well with the learning strategies the student wants to adopt.

These examples illustrate some of the very many obstacles that might arise on placement. Difficulties experienced by a student will not always have a single cause, and several different factors may interact and generate obstacles to learning. A four stage process can be used to help resolve the difficulties.

Identification and recognition
There can be no progress in dealing with an obstacle, unless it is first recognised and identified by both prac-

tice teacher and student. Recognition and identification of an obstacle entails that either practice teacher or student discuss with the other person their concerns about the student's learning. If the practice teacher identifies an obstacle to learning, and then seeks to work on this obstacle without consulting the student, the practice teacher would be operating a covert strategy without the prior agreement of the student. This constitutes unethical practice on the part of the practice teacher. Also, students may be aware of difficulties in some part of the placement system that are adversely affect their learning; unless these difficulties are discussed with the practice teacher, they are unlikely to be resolved. Hence, it is essential that both practice teacher and student jointly acknowledge when an obstacle to learning exits.

Categorisation
Once practice teacher and student have identified the existence of an obstacle to learning, they can mutually explore the precise nature and cause of the obstacle. This will entail an honest discussion, where both exchange their ideas about the possible causes of the obstacle to learning. To do this it is essential to review each of the four elements in the learning environment, so that practice teacher and student can identify the extent to which each element is responsible for generating the obstacle to learning. It is possible that obstacles will have only one cause, however it is equally likely in such a complex system that there will be several different causes each requiring some attention. The obstacle might be a result of these different perceptions of the same situation.

Planning to overcome the obstacle
Having determined where in the system the causes of the obstacle lie, a strategy can be devised by the student and practice teacher to intervene – to remove, avoid or overcome the obstacle. This strategy should be jointly agreed, and decisions made as to who is best able to take action to resolve the difficulty in learning.

Reviewing progress

Once the necessary action has been taken, the practice teacher and student need to review the outcome to ensure that both are satisfied that the obstacle has been dealt with. Depending upon the nature of the obstacle, it may be desirable to have a regular review of the difficulties with learning, to ensure that they do not recur.

Obstacles to learning, if dealt with quickly and effectively, need not adversely affect the placement experience in the long term. They can in themselves form useful learning experiences that enhance the range of strategies for learning.

9

. . . Endings

> Teachers are my lessons done
> or must I learn another one?
> They laughed and laughed: Well
> Child you've only just begun.
> (Leonard Cohen, *Poèmes et chansons*, p. 232)

Summary

Some of the key features of the structured learning model are reviewed, especially how the elements can be combined together. Some suggestions are offered about how not to use the model. Finally, there is some speculation about a desirable future for practice learning.

Making the model work for you

Promoting practice learning is a challenging yet rewarding task for the practice teacher. Likewise for social work students, being on placement is a rigorous exercise in skill development and the acquisition of knowledge and values. It should never be forgotten that on placement students are expected to work in a new area of practice, to develop skills, knowledge and values, and then be examined on their practice competence. All of this occurs within a relatively short period of time, so students and practice teachers need to be realistic about the constraints and possibilities presented by the opportunities for learning on placement. Can we really do what we say we can do and is what we expect of ourselves realistic? Being realistic is a watchword for practice learning. Many practice teachers in the UK work in situations that are not conducive to good practice learning, although considerable changes are in progress. Often, practice teachers work in isolation from each other, receive little acknowledgement of their work as practice teachers, and may still not have the work they do with students recognised as an integral part of their workload. In addition, physical resources may be poor, with access to rooms, books and audio-visual equipment difficult. Yet a substantial number of social work agencies have responded to the challenge of taking practice learning seriously and are devoting resources to enable practice teachers to perform effectively.

Whatever the level of resourcing for practice learning in an agency, individual students must grasp opportunities for learning where they can. Without a recognition by students of the power that they have to shape and influence their own learning they can never achieve their full potential as practitioners. There may be many obstacles, both personal and structural, to the students shaping their own learning. One of the most important steps forward is for students and practice teachers to talk about *how* to maximise learning and to begin to name and recognise any obstacles in the way of achieving desired goals. Once recognised, strategies can be devised to remove or overcome these obstacles.

Putting the pieces together

Each placement represents a unique experience for students and practice teachers. In this book, we have suggested how the placement experience can be structured to promote and enable the student's learning by using what we have termed the structured learning model. This model consists of a series of principles or guidelines that refer to different elements of the placement. Using these principles, it is possible for students and practice teachers together to construct an approach to practice learning. Therefore, each interpretation of the model is unique and is likely to emphasise different elements; nor is it necessary that all of the elements of the practice learning model are incorporated into any one placement. If desired, only some of the elements of the model need be used. It is therefore for practice teachers and students to decide which elements of the model to select and incorporate into their approach to practice learning.

It may be difficult for practice teachers to implement all of the dimensions of this model, even if they wish to do so. Developing and implementing a model of practice learning is not something that can be achieved on the first placement that a practice teacher provides. It may be necessary to develop some parts of the model first and then other components later. Like building a wall, foundations need to be laid before the coping-stones are added; so it is with the development of an approach to practice learning. It will be uneven – some parts of the 'practice learning wall' will be taller than others, some might be made of different material. Only as the wall takes shape over time is it possible to see the parts that need strengthening or rebuilding. So, it will take time to develop, adapt and customise a model of practice learning, such as the structured learning model, to the particular context in which the practice teacher operates. In advocating this model of practice learning, we recognise that the value of a model is the extent to which it is useful in practice. Only through testing can it be refined and developed.

The structured learning model, if fully implemented, consists of the following elements.

1. The recognition of the existence of a society based upon socially structured difference

The experience of being a learner on placement will be affected by the personal biographies of student and practice teacher. These biographies result from living in a society where socially defined differences can lead to discrimination, oppression and an unfair distribution of scarce resources. Differences in ethnicity should be celebrated and human diversity and culture seen as a source of innovation and creativity. Socially structured difference is integral to all elements of practice learning: the relationship of practice teacher and student; the organisational structure of the practice agency and the content of what the student does and learns on placement.

This context for learning is not unique to the structured learning model; it is or ought to be common to all models of practice learning.

Four different elements interact with this learning context to generate the structured learning model, these are as follows.

2. *The importance of learning*

The model incorporates an appreciation of the differing ways in which people approach the task of learning. It is suggested that practice teachers and students need an understanding both of what learning is and how they each approach the learning task. Hence the following three principles are suggested.

Principle one
The structured learning model is grounded on a belief in the importance of educational principles and philosophies. These encompass a wide range of different theories and models. Individual practice teachers and students need to evaluate their own orientation to these different principles and to decide how to incorporate them into their approach to learning.

Principle two
Individuals use different learning strategies when approaching any learning task (Pask, 1976). If students are to get the best out of their learning, they need to develop a wide range of learning strategies that will allow them to learn from the breadth of opportunities available as part of the placement. A task for the practice teacher is to help students to develop competence in a range of learning

strategies. It is easy to make an assumption that students arrive on placement with skills in learning; however, practice teachers need, initially, to help students identify the learning skills that they possess, and then to work jointly with the student to devise ways of building on existing learning strategies and developing new ones.

Principle three
In helping students to develop their learning strategies, full account must be taken of their past experiences of learning. These need to be understood in the context of the students' personal biographies and their experience of socially structured difference.

3. Curriculum

At the heart of the structured learning model is the use of an explicit practice curriculum. Without a curriculum, which may take many forms, the experience of the student on placement is likely to be unstructured and random. Practice teachers usually operate with a curriculum of some sort, whether this is explicit or hidden. The curriculum must be explicit and available before the start of the placement if it is to be of any value to students' learning. This gives student and practice teacher joint access to the curriculum 'map', which will guide the learning throughout the placement. The practice curriculum provides a mechanism to: promote discussion of sequences or patterns of learning on placement; recognise when learning in given areas has been achieved; and ensure that all required areas of learning are addressed during the placement. Practice teachers and students may have a practice curriculum presented for them by the social work programme of which they are a part, or they may need to devise their own.

4. Methods

The model encourages the development of creative and innovative approaches to learning. Also, the model suggests that, when considering which methods of learning to use, practice teachers and students must have regard to: the influence of socially structured difference; the student's learning strategies; and the content to be learned. The decision about *how* to learn any particular area of practice remains a challenge for practice teacher and student. In this decision lies the opportunity for true creativity for students and practice teachers in promoting learning. To help make this decision the structured learning model suggests four principles to be used when selecting any particular method of learning. These are as follows.

Harmony
There needs to be harmony between the method of learning selected and the learning task itself. There is harmony between a method of learning and the skill, knowledge or values to be learned, when the required skill, knowledge or values can be acquired through the method selected.

Effectiveness
Effectiveness of learning is a complex notion. It is not a mechanistic question of measuring a given 'quantity' of learning as plotted against the time invested by the student to produce a desired 'learning outcome'. Effective learning must also take account of the *quality* of learning, which is difficult to define. Perhaps it can be understood using indicators such as: the learner's appraisal of the impact of any learning opportunity; the degree of comprehension; and the likelihood of retention and potential for influencing practice.

Efficiency
It is important for practice teachers to be mindful of the need to teach efficiently, to think carefully about how they use the time available for promoting and enabling learning. This does imply that where face-to-face teaching is undertaken effective use of time is made. Tasks should not be undertaken as joint face-to-face activities if these can be performed equally well by the student outside the practice tutorial, perhaps involving other colleagues. The

notion of *accelerated learning* is a useful one in this context (Doel, 1988).

Linkage to curriculum
The adoption and use of an explicit practice curriculum helps to make the use of methods of learning more systematic; it allows for better pre-planning and selection of particular learning methods, which can be linked to specific modules or units of the curriculum to enable a wide variety of learning methods to be incorporated into the placement.

5. Examination

The structured learning model proposes that students' practice competence should be examined using three principles that together serve as a guide. These principles are:

Principle one: the selection principle

> The nature of the skill, knowledge in practice or value to be examined is the major factor in determining the selection of the method of examination of practice competence.

Some areas of practice can be best measured using particular examination methods. There is a relationship between the type of practice area to be examined and the ways in which it may be effectively measured; moreover, the method of the examination will also influence the nature of learning by the student. As far as possible, when devising methods of examination for practice learning, it is highly desirable if the method selected is one that both promotes and reinforces desirable learning, as well as providing a reliable indicator of practice competence.

Principle two: the correspondence principle

> Correspondences between different pieces of evidence will indicate the actual level of student competence.

The correspondence principle suggests a way of gathering evidence about a student's abilities and how different pieces of evidence can be reconciled with each other.

Principle three: the sampling principle

> Examination events should be distributed throughout a placement on an agreed schedule to sample practice effectively.

Students have a right to know how and when they will be examined on particular aspects of their practice competence. Different components of practice can be best measured by sampling them at different points in the placement. Hence, the examination of practice competence need not be left until the last part of the placement.

The synthesis

Some models prescribe a correct sequence of events, but the structured learning model does not have a series of steps which must be followed in sequential order. This model consists of a series of elements which – when united – define the model. The fusing of the different elements – the recognition that social work is practised in societies dominated by socially structured difference; the use of theories about the way that people learn; the incorporation of a practice curriculum; the use of a wide range of methods of learning; and examination selected according to explicit principles – creates the structured learning model. The use of these elements of the model provides a framework for practice teachers and student to use to help promote students' learning. When the elements are united and used on a placement they jointly reinforce each other to strengthen the quality of the placement and enhance learning. However, any one of the elements of the model may be implemented during a placement, with the practice teacher and student determining how to use these elements and the relative weight to give to them. Practice teachers may wish to experiment with the implementation of the model over several placements.

Towards the future for practice learning

It can be dangerous to speculate on what the future might hold, because predictions go wrong. Rather than seek to second-guess, we will offer some thoughts on how the future of practice learning *might* be, and what we would wish to see:

- *A larger number of practice teachers choosing to remain as practice teachers for a longer period of time* The ability to promote a student's learning requires the accumulation of experience, and it is unfortunate if a substantial number of practice teachers teach one or at most two students before moving on to specialise in other forms of social work practice or management.

- *Practice teachers seeing themselves as practice teachers even when they do not have a student on placement* Practice teachers need time to reflect, prepare and evaluate so that they can develop their teaching for the next student. This is similar to the time college teachers spend in research and preparation, and they consider themselves to be teachers even when the students are not present.

- *The growth in numbers of specialist or semi-specialist practice teachers being seen to represent a great step forward* This growth gives the opportunity for the development of a consistent body of experienced teachers who can focus on practice learning.

- *More examples of good and innovative approaches to practice learning being collected and widely shared* There is tremendous expertise among existing practice teachers and many are using creative forms of learning. Hopefully, the reticence to make these widely available – even to publish them – will be overcome. The development of new teaching material can be very rewarding, and the effort involved in producing new material can be shared between colleagues. For example, if eight practice teachers working in a group devise a piece of simulated learning – an exercise, video, trigger, for example – and share the results, each practice teacher has seven more pieces of material than if they had worked alone. Collective action can be taken further if resource banks are set up in convenient locations. These can also be available to students as self-access learning resources.

- *Forms of partnership between learning in the class and in the agency being further developed*   The current organisation of programmes in the UK is designed with this in mind, yet there is a need for the practice teacher and the college teacher to become true colleagues and equals, so that both have a role in planning and developing learning which is genuinely mutual. One way to achieve this is for practice teachers to work more exclusively with one educational institution and to develop a real knowledge about one programme.

Coda

Human beings are innately curious about the world. Social workers have chosen to exercise that curiosity by trying to understand the experience of other people and help them achieve their aspirations. It is a noble quest, often frustrated by the rigidity of social structures and organisations. If ever social workers lose their passion for fighting injustice and promoting the cause of others, then they are truly lost. However, it can be immensely difficult to retain the spark that keeps the social worker in touch with practice excellence, especially in the face of the vagaries of social work fashion. The spark can be snuffed out early. Through high quality opportunities for practice learning this spark can be fanned and strengthened to a flame for the future by the development of knowledge, values and skills, and the promotion of practice learning on placement.

Most of all, learning should be enjoyable if it is to excite and stimulate the student; something has gone very wrong if it becomes a burden. Hence, our final comment for students and practice teachers is:

. . . have fun and learn!

References

Ahmad, B. (1990) *Black Perspectives in Social Work*, Birmingham, Venture Press.

Ahmed, S. (1987) 'Let's Break through the Business to Equality', *Community Care*, 684, inside supplement i–iii.

Akhurst, C. (1978) 'Assessment of Performance in Professional Practice in Social Work Courses', *Assessment in Higher Education*, vol. 4, no. 1, pp. 46–59.

Arkava, M. L. and Brennen, E. C. (eds) (1976) *Competency-Based Education for Social Work*, New York, Council on Social Work Education.

Badger, D. (1991) 'Assessment of Practice Competence: The experience of the viva voce: A case study', *Issues in Social Work Education*, vol. 11, no. 1, pp. 3–22.

Baird, P. (1991) 'The Proof of the Pudding: A study of client views of student practice competence', *Issues in Social Work Education*, vol. 10, nos 1 and 2, pp. 24–41.

BASW (1986) *A Code of Ethics for Social Work* (revised edn), Birmingham, British Association of Social Workers.

Biggs, S. (1990) 'Ageism and Confronting Ageing: Experiential groupwork to examine attitudes to older age', *Journal of Social Work Practice*, vol. 4, no. 2, pp. 49–65.

Bogo, M. and Vayda, E. (1987) *The Practice of Field Instruction in Social Work*, Toronto, University of Toronto Press.

Borland, M., Hudson, A., Hughes, B. and Worrall, A. (1988) 'An Approach to the Management of Practice Placements', *British Journal of Social Work*, vol. 18, no. 3, pp. 269–88.

Boud, D., Cohen, R. and Walker, D. (1993) *Using Experience of Learning*, Milton Keynes, Society for Research into Higher Education and Open University Press.

Boyne, R. and Rattansi, A. (1990) *Postmodernism and Society*, London, Macmillan.

Brandon, J. and Davies, M. (1979) 'The Limits of Competence in Social Work: The assessment of marginal students in social work education', *British Journal of Social Work*, vol. 9, no. 3, pp. 295–348.

Bruner, J. (1966) *Toward a Theory of Instruction*, Cambridge, Mass, The Belknap Press of Harvard University.

Butler, B. and Elliot, D. (1985) *Teaching and Learning for Practice*, Aldershot, Gower.

Buzan, T. (1974) *Use Your Head*, London, BBC Publications.

CCETSW (1989) *Requirements and Regulations for the Diploma in Social Work (Paper 30)*, London, Central Council for Education and Training in Social Work.

CCETSW (1991a) *One Small Step Towards Racial Justice*, London, Central Council for Education and Training in Social Work.

CCETSW (1991a) *Requirements and Guidance for the Approval of Agencies and the Accreditation and Training of Practice Teachers (Paper 26.3)* (revised edn), London, Central Council for Education and Training in Social Work.

CCETSW (1991b) *Rules and Requirements for the Diploma in Social Work (Paper 30)* (second edn), London, Central Council for Education and Training in Social Work.

CCETSW (1992) *The Requirements for Post Qualifying Education and Training in the Personal Social Services (Paper 31)* (revised edn), London, Central Council for Education and Training in Social Work.

Chinnery, B. (1990) 'The Process of Being Disabled', *Practice*, vol. 4, no. 1, pp. 43–8.

Clark, F. W. (1976) 'The Competency-Based Curriculum', in Arkava, M. L. and Brennen, E. C. (eds) *Competency-Based Education for Social Work*, New York, Council on Social Work Education, pp. 22–46.

Coulshed, V. (1989) 'Developing the Process Curriculum', *Issues in Social Work Education*, vol. 9, nos. 1 and 2, pp. 21–30.

Cox, R. E. (1982) 'The Educational Expectations of Social Work Students', *British Journal of Social Work*, vol. 12, no. 3, pp. 381–94.

Cross, T. L., Bazron, B. J., Dennis, K. W. and Isaacs, M. R. (1989) *Towards a Culturally Competent System of Care*, Washington DC, CASSP Technical Assistance Center.

Curry, L. (1983) *Learning Style in Continuing Medical Education*, Ottawa, Council on Medical Education, Canadian Medical Association.

Danbury, H. (1986) *Teaching Practical Social Work* (2nd edn), Aldershot, Gower.

Davies, M. (1984a) *The Essential Social Worker* (2nd edn), Aldershot, Gower.

Davies, M. (1984b) 'Training: What we think of it now', *Social*

Work Today, vol. 15, no. 20, pp. 12–17.

de Galle, H. (1991) 'Black Students Views of Existing CQSW Courses and CSS Schemes 2', in CDPS Group (eds) *Setting the Context for Change*, London, Central Council for Education and Training in Social Work, pp. 101–12.

Devore, W. and Schlesinger, E. G. (1991) *Ethnic-Sensitive Social Work Practice* (3rd edn), Columbus, Ohio, Macmillan.

Doel, M. (1987a) 'The Practice Curriculum', *Social Work Education*, vol. 6, no. 3, pp. 6–12.

Doel, M. (1987b) 'Putting the "Final" in the Final Report', *Social Work Today*, vol. 18, no. 22, pp. 13.

Doel, M. (1988) 'A Practice Curriculum to Promote Accelerated Learning', in Phillipson, J., Richards, M. and Sawdon, D. (eds), *Towards a Practice Led Curriculum*, London, National Institute for Social Work, pp. 45–60.

Doel, M. (1990) 'Putting Heart into the Curriculum', *Community Care*, no. 797, pp. 20–2.

Doel, M. and Marsh, P. (1992) *Task-Centred Social Work*, Aldershot, Ashgate.

Doel, M. and Shardlow, S. M. (1989) 'Teaching Social Work Practice by Assignment', *Issues in Social Work Education*, vol. 9, nos 1 and 2, pp. 53–73.

Doel, M. and Shardlow, S. M. (1993) *Social Work Practice*, Aldershot, Gower.

Doel, M. and Shardlow S. M. (1996) *Teaching Social Work Practice*, Aldershot, Arena.

England, H. (1986) *Social Work as Art*, London, Allen & Unwin.

Entwistle, N. (1978) 'Knowledge Structures and Styles of Learning: A summary of Pask's recent research', *British Journal of Educational Psychology*, vol. 48, pp. 255–65.

Evans, D. (1987) 'Live Supervision in the Same Room: A practice teaching method', *Social Work Education*, vol. 6, no. 3, pp. 13–17.

Evans, D. (1991) *Assessing Students' Competence to Practice*, London, Central Council for Education and Training in Social Work.

Ford, K. and Jones, A. (1987) *Student Supervision*, London, Macmillan.

Furniss, J. (1988) 'The Client Speaks Again', *Profile*, vol. 3, pp. 2–3.

Gagné, R. M. (1972) 'Domains of Learning', *Interchange*, vol. 3, no. 1, pp. 1–8.

Gardiner, D. (1989) *The Anatomy of Supervision*, Milton Keynes, The Society for Research into Higher Education and Open University Press.

George, A. (1982) 'A History of Social Work Field Instruction', in Sheafor, B. W. and Jenkins, L. E. (eds), *Quality Field Instruction in Social Work*, New York, Longman, pp. 37–59.

Goodall, J. and Lenn, M. (1984) 'A Task Based Approach to the Assessment of Social Work Students' Practice', *British Journal of Social Work*, vol. 14, no. 3, pp. 211–25.

Grundy, S. (1987) *Curriculum: Product or Praxis?* Lewes, East Sussex, The Falmer Press.

Hayward, C. (1979) *A Fair Assessment*, London, Central Council for Education and Training in Social Work.

Hirst, P. H. (1969) 'The Logic of the Curriculum', *Journal of Curriculum Studies*, vol. 1, no. 2, pp. 142–58.

Holden, W. (1972) 'Process Recording', *Social Work Education Reporter*, vol. 20, pp. 67–9.

Honey, P. and Mumford, A. (1986) *The Manual of Learning Styles*, Maidenhead, Ardingly House.

Howe, D. (1987) *An Introduction to Social Work Theory*, Aldershot, Wildwood House.

Hudson, B. L. and Macdonald, G. M. (1986) *Behavioural Social Work*, London, Macmillan.

Humphries, B. (1988) 'Adult Learning in Social Work Education: Towards liberation or domestication', *Critical Social Policy*, vol. 23, pp. 8–21.

Humphries, B., Pankhania-Wimmer, H., Seale, A. and Stokes, I. (eds) (1993) *Improving Practice Teaching and Learning*, Leeds, Northern Curriculum Development Project, Central Council for Education and Training.

IFSW (1988) *International Code of Ethics for the Professional Social Worker*, Vienna, International Federation of Social Workers.

Illich, I. D. (1971) *Deschooling Society*, London, Calder & Boyars.

ILPS (1993) *Working with Difference*, London, Inner London Probation Service.

Johnson, D. W. (1993) *Reaching Out* (5th edn), Needham Heights, Mass., Allyn & Bacon.

Kadushin, A. (1973) *Supervision in Social Work*, New York, Columbia University Press.

Kelly, A. V. (1989) *The Curriculum: Theory and Practice* (3rd edn), London, Paul Chapman.

Kerr, B. (1988) '"Durham Revisited". Further Thoughts on Consistency and Standards in Assessment for a Social Work Qualification', *Social Work Education*, vol. 7, no. 2, pp. 19–23.

Kidd, J. R. (1973) *How Adults Learn*, New York, Association Press.

Knowles, M. (1970) *The Modern Practice of Adult Education*, New York, Association Press.

Knowles, M. (1972) 'Innovations in Teaching Styles and Approaches Based on Adult Learning', *Journal of Education for Social Work*, vol. 8, no. 2, pp. 32–9.

Kolb, D. (1976) *Learning Styles Inventory Technical Manual*, Boston, Mass., McBer.

Kuhn, T. S. (1970) 'The Structure of Scientific Revolutions', in Neurath, O., Carnap, R. and C. Morris (eds), *Foundations of the Unity of Science: Toward an International Encyclopedia of Unified Science*, Chicago, University of Chicago Press, pp. 54–272.

Kutzik, A. J. (1977) 'The Social Work Field', in Kaslow, F. W. and Associates (eds) *Supervision, Consultation and Staff Training in the Helping Professions*, San Francisco, Jossey-Bass, pp. 25–9.

Lewin, K. (1948) *Resolving Social Conflicts*, New York, Harper & Brothers.

Lovell, R. B. (1980) *Adult Learning*, London, Croom Helm.

Macdonald, J. B. and Macdonald, S. C. (1988) 'Gender, Values and Curriculum', in Pinar, W. F. (eds) *Contemporary Curriculum Discourses*, Scottsdale, Arizona, Gorsuch Scarisbrick, pp. 476–85.

Megginson, D. and Boydell, T. (1989) *A Manager's Guide to Coaching*, London, British Assocation for Commercial and Industrial Education (BACIE).

Meinert, R. G. (1972) 'Simulation Technology: A potential tool for social work education', *Journal of Education for Social Work*, vol. 8, no. 3, pp. 50–90.

Millard, D. W. (1972) 'The Examination of Students' Fieldwork', *Social Work Today*, vol. 3, no. 14, pp. 13–6.

Millard, D. W. (1978) 'Fieldwork Evaluation Revisited', *British Journal of Social Work*, vol. 8, no. 1, pp. 71–7.

Minty, B., Glynn, E., Huxley, P. and Hamilton, M. (1988) 'The Assessment of Students' Practice', *Social Work Education*, vol. 7, no. 2, pp. 9–14.

Morrell, E. (1980) 'Student Assessment – Where Are We Now?', *British Journal of Social Work*, vol. 10, no. 4, pp. 431–42.

NASW (1990) *Code of Ethics*, Silver Spring, Md, National Association of Social Workers.

Newble, D. I. and Entwistle, N. J. (1986) 'Learning Styles and Approaches: implications for medical education', *Medical Education*, vol. 20, pp. 162–75.

Norman, A. (1985) *Triple Jeopardy: Growing Old in a Second*

Homeland, London, Centre for Policy on Ageing.

Parsloe, P. (1983) 'The Transfer of Skills from Learning to Practice', in CCETSW, *Research in Practice Teaching*, London, Central Council for Education and Training in Social Work, pp. 40–53.

Pask, G. (1976) 'Styles and Strategies of Learning', *British Journal of Educational Psychology*, vol. 46, pp. 128–48.

Payne, M. (1991) *Modern Social Work Theory*, London, Macmillan.

Pettes, D. E. (1967) *Supervision in Social Work*, London, George Allen & Unwin.

Pettes, D. E. (1979) *Staff and Student Supervision: A Task-Centred Approach*, London, George Allen & Unwin.

Phillipson, J. (1992) *Practising Equality: Women, Men and Social Work*, London, Central Council for Education and Training in Social Work.

Phillipson, J., Richards, M. and Sawdon, D. (eds) (1988) *Towards a Practice Led Curriculum*, London, National Institute for Social Work.

Piaget, J. (1953) *The Origins of Intelligence in the Child*, London, Routledge & Kegan Paul.

Reynolds, B. (1942) *Learning and Teaching in the Practice of Social Work*, New York, Rinehart & Company.

Richards, M. (1987) 'Developing the Context of Practice Teaching', *Social Work Education*, vol. 6, no. 2, pp. 4–9.

Richards, M. (1988) 'Developing the Content of Practice Teaching (Part 2)', in Phillipson, J., Richards, M. and Sawdon, D. (eds) *Towards a Practice Led Curriculum*, London, National Institute for Social Work, pp. 69–74.

Richardson, L. B. (1982) 'Survey of Final Fieldwork Placements', *Probation Journal*, vol. 29, no. 2, pp. 54–6.

Rogers, A. (1986) *Teaching Adults*, Milton Keynes, Open University Press.

Rogers, J. (1977) *Adults Learning*, Milton Keynes, Open University Press.

Rosenblatt, A. and Meyer, J. E. (1975) 'Objectionable Supervisory Styles: Students' views', *Social Work*, vol. 20, pp. 184–89.

Rowntree, D. (1976) *Learn How to Study*, London, Macdonald & James.

Rowntree, D. (1991) *Teach Yourself with Open Learning*, Guernsey, Sphere Books.

Sawdon, C. (1985) 'Action Techniques', unpublished paper.

Sawdon, D. T. (1986) *Making Connections in Practice Teaching*, London, National Institute for Social Work.

Shardlow, S. M. (1987) 'Assessing Practice Competence: The first year of a professional practice advisory panel', *Practice*, vol. 1, no. 1, pp. 81–93.

Shardlow, S. M. (1989a) 'Training and Practice: A fantasy', *Social Work Today*, vol. 20, no. 20, p. 36.

Shardlow, S. M. (1989b) 'The Use of Pre-recorded Video on a Course for Practice Teachers', *Social Work Education*, vol. 8, no. 2, pp. 25–32.

Shardlow, S. M. and Doel, M. (1991) 'Verbal Self Report and Direct Observation: Modes of examining practice competence', in Delooz, P., Hiernaux, J. P., Lopez, M. L. and Somze, D. (eds) *Non-Verbal Trends in Social Work*, Liège, Belgium, Ecole Supérieure d'Action Sociale (ESAS), pp. 137–46.

Shardlow, S. M. and Doel, M. (1992a) 'Practice Teaching and Knowledge', *Social Work Education*, vol. 11, no. 3, pp. 45–53.

Shardlow, S. M. and Doel, M. (1992b) 'Towards Anti-Racist Practice Teaching', *Practice*, vol. 6, no. 3, pp. 60–6.

Sheafor, B. W. and Jenkins, L. E. (1982) 'An Overview of Social Work Field Instruction', in Sheafor, B. W. and Jenkins, L. E. (eds) *Quality Field Instruction in Social Work*, New York, Longman, pp. 3–20.

Sheldon, B. and Baird, P. (1978) 'Evaluating Student Performance', *Social Work Today*, vol. 10, no. 16, pp. 15–18.

Siporin, M. (1982) 'The Process of Field Instruction', in Sheafor, B. W. and Jenkins, L. E. (eds) *Quality Field Instruction in Social Work*, New York, Longman, pp. 175–95.

Sockett, H. (1976) *Designing the Curriculum*, London, Open Books.

South Yorkshire DipSW (1993) *Practice One Handbook*, Sheffield, South Yorkshire Diploma in Social Work.

Stenhouse, L. (1975) *An Introduction to Curriculum Research and Development*, London, Heinemann.

Syson, L. and Baginsky, M. (1981) *Learning to Practise: A study of practice placements in courses leading to the Certificate of Qualification in Social Work*, London, Central Council for Education and Training in Social Work.

Thompson, N. (1993) *Anti-Discriminatory Practice*, London, Macmillan.

Thompson, N., Osada, M. and Anderson, B. (1990) *Practice Teaching in Social Work*, Birmingham, PEPAR.

Toussaint, P., Yeardley, A. and Leyden, J. (1989) *Live Supervision*, London, London Borough of Hackney.

Tyler, R. W. (1949) *Basic Principles of Curriculum and Instruction*, Chicago, University of Chicago Press.

Urdang, E. (1979) 'In Defense of Process Recording', *Smith College Studies in Social Work*, vol. 50, no. i, pp. 109–16.

Wijnberg, M. H. and Schwartz, M. C. (1977) 'Models of Student Supervision: The apprenticeship, growth and role systems models', *Journal of Education for Social Work*, vol. 13, no. 3, pp. 107–13.

Wilkie, C. H. (1963) 'A Study of Distortions in Recording Interviews', *Social Work*, vol. 8, no. 3, pp. 31–6.

Wilkinson, J. and Canter, S. (1982) *Social Skills Training Manual*, Chichester, Wiley.

Wilson, S. J. (1981) *Field Instruction*, New York, The Free Press.

Name Index

Subject Index